THE MORMON CHURCH
A BASIC HISTORY

THE MORMON CHURCH
A BASIC HISTORY

by Dean Hughes

Deseret Book Company
Salt Lake City, Utah

For Carl Hurst

First printing in paperbound edition, August 1990

Library of Congress Cataloging-in-Publication Data

Hughes, Dean, 1943–
    The Mormon Church.

    Bibliography: p.
    Includes index.
    1. Church of Jesus Christ of Latter-day Saints —
History. 2. Mormon Church — History. I. Title.
BX8611.H77 1986   289.3′32′09   86-13566
ISBN 0-87579-343-6

Printed in the United States of America

10 9 8 7 6 5 4 3 2 1

Contents

CONTENTS

Preface

The Mormon Church: A Basic History is a beginner's history of The Church of Jesus Christ of Latter-day Saints. It is intended for older children and teenagers, or for anyone who would like to begin a basic study of the Church.

Sources for the book are, for the most part, the many fine published books that deal in greater detail with the periods and complex facets of Mormon history. The bibliography at the end of the book lists most of these sources and can also serve as a useful guide for the person who would like to study the history in depth.

I would like to express my appreciation to Larry C. Porter and David Whittaker, both of Brigham Young University and both respected scholars of Mormon history, who read my manuscript and advised me extensively. I appreciate the careful editorial work of Eleanor Knowles of Deseret Book Company. I also appreciate my children, Tom, Amy, and Robert, and my wife, Kathleen, who were willing to read the manuscript and give helpful criticism.

SECTION I

THE BEGINNINGS

"Mormon" is the name often used for a member of The Church of Jesus Christ of Latter-day Saints. The story of the Mormons begins with miracles—angels and heavenly visions—and yet it begins in the backwoods of New York state. And it begins with a young boy—a farm boy— with the common name of Joseph Smith.

CHAPTER 1

Joseph Smith

In 1820 Joseph Smith, Jr., lived near the small community of Manchester, New York. He was fourteen years old. The house he lived in was simple, built of logs—two rooms on the ground floor and two attic rooms. He had five brothers and two sisters. Alvin, Hyrum, and Sophronia were older than he, and Samuel, William, Catherine, and Don Carlos were younger. The next year another child, Lucy, would come into the world, bringing the number of children to nine.

The Smiths were farmers, but the father and sons also sometimes worked as laborers for other people. Joseph, Sr., and his wife, Lucy Mack, had started married life fairly well off, but a swindler had cheated them out of a large sum of money, and they had lost their first farm. Over the next couple of decades they had scratched out a living on New England and New York farms or by whatever work they could find.

Lucy had done everything from selling baked goods and homemade root beer to painting oilcloths for table coverings. Joseph, Sr., took work as a cooper at times, making buckets and barrels, and he also dug and then rocked up wells and basement walls. The children helped by selling cakes and gingerbread from a pushcart on any occasion that caused a crowd to gather in the area. They also helped to make brooms and baskets, and to cut firewood to sell.

Lucy was known for her "doctoring," although she probably did not do this for money. One neighbor said that no one was better than the Smiths to help out when someone was sick.

Joseph, Jr., spent almost all his time on the farm with his family. He did attend school sometimes during the winter months, but most of the year he worked in the fields. The closest town of any size was Palmyra, which had fewer than four thousand people. It was an active, growing town on the Erie Canal, with blacksmith and tailor shops, tanneries, sawmills, taverns, and a hotel. But Joseph did not spend much time there. There was too much work to do on the farm.

Few people in the backwoods of western New York were formally educated. Though Joseph learned the basics of reading and writing—more from his parents than from school—he knew little grammar, and his spelling was mostly guesswork. He was not studious as a boy. His mother noted that he almost never read the scriptures in his early years. A vigorous, fun-loving young man, he had bright blue eyes and blond hair. And he was sturdy, with wide shoulders and muscular arms.

When the Smith family arrived in Manchester in 1818, Joseph worked with his father and brothers to clear the land for their farm. They hacked away the underbrush and grubbed out the small trees, cutting the large ones and dragging them off. Then they plowed around the stumps. They prepared close to thirty acres of land in one year. It was a huge undertaking that must have kept them busy from sunup until sundown for many months. They also harvested sugar from hundreds of maple trees, reaping as much as a thousand pounds a year. It is not surprising that Joseph found little time to study or to read the scriptures.

The Smiths were religious, but they did not belong to any church for a long time. Joseph, Sr., considered himself a "seeker," someone who was searching for the truth but had not found it in any church. Lucy was a member of the Presbyterian Church for a time.

Religious revivals were common in rural New York, with preachers traveling from town to town to hold outdoor camp meetings. Their preaching was fiery, as they called the people to repentance and warned them against the pains of hell. Young Joseph attended some of these meetings, and he watched others become overwhelmed, even wild, as they were moved by the sermons. He wanted conversion, to know God's truths, but he was not moved by the camp meetings. He wished that he could shout with the joy of the Spirit, as many others did, but in honesty he felt no such joy.

All the same, he was a thoughtful boy, and eventually he began to study the Bible on his own. He came to regret his own sins and the sins of a wicked world. He wondered whether he could be forgiven. He also wondered whether he should join any of the churches he had visited or heard about.

Then he came across a particular passage in the book of James in the New Testament. He read: "If any of you lack wisdom, let him ask of God, that giveth to all men liberally, and upbraideth not; and it shall be given him." (James 1:5.) The scripture entered Joseph's heart with "great force." He decided that he must ask God directly for answers to his questions.

On a spring morning in 1820, when the weather had turned mild, Joseph went to the woods not far from his home. He knelt in a little grove, among the hickory and oak trees, and began to pray. Soon he felt a power come over him. It bound up his tongue and filled him with fear. He heard noises about him and a thick darkness descended. He felt almost consumed with fear and the darkness, but he continued to pray. Then a light appeared, brighter than the sun, and the light descended and encircled him. Looking up, he saw two personages, dressed in white robes, their brightness and beauty beyond his ability to describe. One of them pointed to the other and said, "This is My Beloved Son. Hear Him!"

Joseph Smith's first vision

Joseph received the answer to his concern about his sins, for he was told, "Joseph my son, thy sins are forgiven thee." He felt himself accepted by the Lord, finally awakened in spirit, as he had hoped to become.

In answer to Joseph's other question, the Son of God told him that he should join no church, for the churches of the world had become corrupt: "They draw near to me with their lips, but their hearts are far from me, they teach for doctrines the commandments of men, having a form of godliness, but they deny the power thereof." Joseph was then promised that at some time the fullness of the gospel would be made known to him.

Joseph was just a boy, fourteen years old. But he had seen the Father and the Son; he had heard their voices. As he walked from the grove, he was weak, still stunned by what he had experienced. He knew that much would be expected of him now, and that God had some purpose for him. He could never be an ordinary boy again.

And yet, in most ways he was an ordinary boy. He was inexperienced, had had very little formal education, and certainly was not a Bible scholar. Would anyone ever believe what had happened to him? He soon found out the answer to that question. Most did not believe him. He told his story to a minister, who exploded in anger and accused Joseph of making it up. He told a few others, and it was not long until he was persecuted by adults and teased by boys his own age.

But members of his family believed him. They knew him. They heard his simple story and felt that it was true. They encouraged him to be worthy of what God would have in store for him.

Three years later, on Sunday night, September 21, 1823, Joseph lay in bed. He was feeling remorseful, unworthy. He knew that he had made the kinds of mistakes that other boys made, and he prayed to the Lord for forgiveness. He hoped that he could once again be assured that God loved him.

The room began to grow light. Everything around him became intensely bright, and then an angel appeared, standing above the floor. The glorious person, dressed in a brilliant white robe, spoke, saying that his name was Moroni. He assured Joseph that his sins were forgiven and that God still loved him.

Moroni said that Joseph had a great work to do and that his name would be known for both good and evil throughout the world. He could expect many to hate him and work against him, but the work must be done. He then told Joseph about a book written upon plates having the "appearance of gold." The book was an account of a people who had formerly lived on the American continent. It was also a record of scripture, containing the "fulness of the everlasting gospel." Joseph was to translate these records with the help of two "seer stones" that he would receive with the plates.

Moroni gave Joseph many other instructions and then told him that his work was to help the world prepare for the second coming of Christ. Once he received the plates, he must carry out the work, but he must not show the plates to anyone else.

The brightness then gathered around Moroni, and he ascended from the room. Joseph lay back, marveling at what had happened, but he had little time to think. Within moments, the vision opened again. Moroni returned and repeated the instructions, adding new information. Again he ascended—and a third time he returned, repeating and enlarging on what he had said before. This time Moroni warned Joseph that he must not seek worldly gain through the plates, but must use them to glorify God.

The visions lasted all night. At daybreak Joseph got up and went out to do his usual work in the fields. He was tired and weak, however, and his father, seeing this, sent him to the house. But as Joseph attempted to cross a fence on the way, he fainted. Suddenly Moroni reappeared and repeated everything he had told Joseph the night before. This time he also told Joseph to return to his father and to tell him all that he had seen and heard.

Joseph was afraid. What if his father didn't believe him? But his father felt the sincerity and truth of the story, and told Joseph to do exactly as the angel had instructed him.

During the angel's appearance, Joseph had seen a vision of the spot where the plates were buried. It was near the crest of a hill not far from the family farm. Now Joseph went to the hill and found the place. He uncovered a stone box, and in it he saw the gold plates and a metal breastplate. With the breastplate were the "Urim and Thummim," the seer stones.

Joseph reached for the plates, but the messenger, the angel Moroni, appeared again and told him not to take them yet. Joseph later admitted that the sight of the gold, to a poor farm boy, was almost too tempting, and that for a moment he lost sight of his mission. The angel scolded him for having such thoughts.

Moroni then told Joseph that he could not take the plates yet. He must first prove himself worthy. He must return at the same time the next year to receive further instructions.

Joseph went home. That night he sat with his family and recounted every detail of what he had experienced. Many years later, his brother William remembered that evening. He said, "The whole family were melted in tears, and believed all he said. Knowing that he was very young, that he had not enjoyed the advantages of a common education; and knowing too, his whole character and disposition, they were convinced that he was totally incapable of arising before his aged parents, his brothers and sisters, and so solemnly giving utterance to anything but the truth."

Two months later, Joseph's eldest brother, Alvin, became critically ill. No one was more pleased or confident about young Joseph's calling than Alvin, and Joseph loved no one more than this brother.

The Smiths had a large family to provide for, and now the eldest, the strongest, the one they had depended on the most, was dying. A doctor had given Alvin calomel, a powerful medicine that was supposed to make him well. Instead, it was killing him.

Medicine in those days was a crude art. Joseph knew all about that. Before he had turned eight, he also had been critically ill. A doctor had opened up his infected leg and, without giving him any kind of painkiller, had scraped out the infection and then chiseled away pieces of bone. His leg had been saved, but Joseph had suffered terribly, and he still walked with a slight limp.

Now it seemed overwhelming for Joseph to accept that his brother would die. As Alvin lay in his bed, he spoke to members of his family. He told Hyrum, the next oldest brother, to take care of their parents and to finish the larger house that he, Alvin, had begun to build. He spoke also to other family members, but it was Joseph who received the greatest attention. He told Joseph to be a good boy and to do everything in his power to obtain the promised plates. Joseph held his brother's hand and vowed to do so.

The gold plates. Joseph must live worthy to receive them. It was what the whole family expected of him. The powerful and kindly Alvin had heard his little brother's account of his visions, and he believed him. Joseph knew he must live up to what he had been called to do. He had made a promise to Alvin, but, more than that, he had promised God.

CHAPTER 2

The Gold Plates

Joseph had been told that he must wait four years to receive the plates. The next few years were difficult for him, full of expectancy, and yet long years for a young man to wait and go about his work on the family farm. He was not entirely isolated, however. He joined a young person's debating society, talked religion with many neighbors, and read the Palmyra newspaper every week. He also did farm work for neighbors or chores for families in town to add to his family's income.

Farming was hard work at that time. Teams of oxen pulled large "bull plows," which quickly became dull and had to be sharpened. A farmer had to have strength to guide the plows, especially in newly broken land. Joseph learned to plow and to dig wells, and he became physically strong. He acquired a reputation as an almost unbeatable wrestler. His favorite game was pulling sticks. Two people sat opposite each other, the bottoms of their feet together. Then both grasped a stick and pulled, trying to raise the other to his feet. Joseph was eventually known to pull two strong men to their feet, or using just one arm, to handle one.

Years later Joseph would look back on these four years

without much pride, feeling that he had been too much like other young men and not serious enough about his calling. He also came to feel that he had done things that had not improved his own or his family's reputation. He had perhaps told too many people about his visions, and the story had been widely repeated, often in exaggerated forms.

Western New Yorkers, like many rural Americans of the time, were steeped in superstition and folk magic. Just as some people today believe in "water witching," so many people in that day believed that certain sorts of sticks could be used as divining rods to discover hidden treasure. "Peep stones" were used for the same purpose. Many people encouraged Joseph to believe that because of his visions, he could use such devices to find money or treasure.

In 1825 a man named Josiah Stowell visited Joseph and asked him to help dig for some Spanish silver believed to be hidden in an abandoned mine. Mr. Stowell had heard of Joseph's spiritual experiences, and he thought that Joseph could divine the place where the silver was hidden.

At this time Joseph may have been wondering how he would be allowed to use his spiritual gifts. He seemed to believe, as did many of his neighbors, that there was something to the magical devices. And now a man was offering him high wages—fourteen dollars a week—to come and help dig for treasure. The Smiths had struggled since Alvin's death to meet the mortgage payments on their house—the house that Alvin had begun and the family had now almost finished. Money was always hard to come by, so this was an opportunity to make some.

The abandoned mine was in Harmony, in the Susquehannah valley of Pennsylvania, just across the New York state line. Joseph, who was accompanied by his father, attempted to find the treasure, but he was not successful. After a month he convinced Mr. Stowell to give up the search. He

remained in the area to work for Mr. Stowell as well as a
family named Knight, who lived nearby in Broome County,
New York.

Josiah Stowell and Joseph Knight both thought very
highly of Joseph Smith. Mr. Knight described Joseph as the
best hand he had ever employed. But others were more criti-
cal of the "money digging" Joseph had been involved in.
The incident was brought up time and again throughout his
life as "proof" against his character.

For Joseph, however, the incident was a learning experience. He began to understand that the gifts God had given
him were not intended to make him and his family wealthy.
By 1827, when the time came to begin the translation of the
plates, he was ready to work for much higher purposes.

Something else of great value came of the excursion into
Pennsylvania. It was there that Joseph met Emma Hale, the
young woman who became his wife. When Joseph and his
father went to work for Josiah Stowell, they boarded with
the Isaac Hale family, and it was there that Joseph and
Emma became acquainted.

By now Joseph was tall and muscular. He had a presence
about him—a growing confidence and an outgoing friend-
liness—that attracted people. But Emma was apparently
attracted by more than his good looks. During their early ac-
quaintance he told her about the experiences he had had—
the visions and the promise to receive the plates. Though
Emma was a religious young woman, she might have been
skeptical of such a story. But she believed Joseph and felt the
honesty and sincerity in his account.

Emma was a year older than Joseph. A tall, striking
woman, with dark hair and hazel eyes, she was gracious and
reserved but also confident and strong-willed. When Joseph
proposed to her, she was willing to marry him in spite of his
poverty. However, her father was opposed. In Mr. Hale's

mind, Joseph was a visionary, a "money digger"—not some-one Emma should put her trust in.

Joseph waited a few months and then asked Isaac Hale again for permission to marry Emma. Again Mr. Hale re-fused. The third time Joseph proposed to Emma, she ac-cepted, but this time she did not tell her father. Joseph and Emma were married, and he took her back to his family farm near Manchester. After a time she became partially recon-ciled with her father, but he was never very enthusiastic about Joseph or the life that Emma had chosen to share with him.

Joseph worked on his father's farm that year. He strug-gled to make the best life possible for his new wife. Then one day he went into Manchester to take care of some business. He didn't return by nightfall, as expected. When he finally arrived home, he was exhausted and didn't speak for some time. Finally he explained what had happened.

"I have taken the severest chastisement that I have ever had," he said. The angel Moroni, the same messenger who had appeared to him before, had suddenly confronted him as he passed by the hill where the plates were hidden. He told Joseph that he had "not been engaged enough in the work of the Lord." The time had come for Joseph to receive the plates and begin his work.

Shortly after midnight, in the early hours of September 22, 1827, Joseph and Emma went to the hill, whose name they learned was Cumorah. Joseph was careful to go by night, fearing that he might be followed otherwise. Many knew about his agreement with Moroni and hoped to beat Joseph to what they thought was a great treasure.

Joseph left Emma in the wagon they had borrowed, and he climbed the hill. The north side was grassy and steep, but the plates were buried among some trees near the top and on the west side. When he returned to the wagon, Emma saw

Joseph Smith
receives the gold
plates

that he was carrying something heavy wrapped in his cloak. He got into the wagon and they hastened away. In the woods he stopped the horses and took the plates to a hollow log, where he hid them. He knew people would be watching for him, and he dared not take the plates home yet.

When Joseph and Emma finally arrived home, after breakfast, Joseph calmed his mother, told her all was well, and let her hold the seer stones, the interpreters. She later described them. They were wrapped in a silk handkerchief, she said, but there seemed to be two stones, "like smooth, three-cornered diamonds set in glass," and they were fixed in frames like old-fashioned spectacles.

Joseph needed a proper box to lock the plates in, but he had no money for such a purchase. The next day he learned of a well-digging job, and he went to the town of Macedon to take the job and earn the needed money.

However, word was getting around that Joseph Smith

had a "gold bible" at his place. Men began to search the farm at night, trying to find the plates. Emma rode on horseback to Macedon to tell Joseph of the danger, and he returned with her. It was time, he said, to bring the plates home and to protect them properly.

Joseph left that night on foot, trudging through the woods, still wearing the linen smock he had worn while digging the well. He got the plates from the hollow log, wrapped them in the smock, and started back. When he failed to return home soon, his family became worried. Finally he arrived, tired and dirty, and with his thumb injured. The plates were very heavy—perhaps sixty pounds—and so

Joseph Smith returning home with the gold plates

the going had not been easy. In addition, he had been attacked three times that night by men lying in wait for him, but each time he had been able to get away. One of the attackers had struck him with a gun, but Joseph's extraordinary strength saved him. He knocked the man down and escaped. Then he had carried the heavy plates the entire three miles.

Joseph borrowed a cherry-wood chest from his married brother, Hyrum, and put the plates inside. Then he removed some stones from the hearth of the fireplace and buried the box beneath them. He had just replaced the stones when some armed men showed up. Thinking quickly, Joseph told those in the house to run out the door, screaming and yelling. This surprised the men outside and scared them away.

But Joseph's troubles were not over. He realized that he could not translate the plates under such conditions. He would have to go somewhere else. It was at this point that Martin Harris, a man who knew Joseph and believed in his calling, came to help. He gave Joseph fifty dollars, making it possible for him to take Emma and to return to her home in Pennsylvania. The fifty dollars would hold them over for a time.

CHAPTER 3

The Book of Mormon

Joseph and Emma did not receive a warm welcome at the home of Isaac Hale. He was furious that Joseph would not allow him to see the plates. All the same, he allowed Joseph and Emma to move into a small house on his farm. Joseph agreed to pay two hundred dollars for thirteen acres of land to farm, and Mr. Hale did not press for immediate payment. The house had just three rooms, and Joseph did his translating in the attic room, lighted by a window facing the east.

And so the work began. Over the next several months the record on the plates, a record of ancient peoples who had inhabited the American continent many centuries ago, would be translated and then published as a sacred volume of scripture, the Book of Mormon.

Joseph knew nothing about languages or translation, and he soon learned that the interpreter stones did not provide him with a simple word-for-word account. He had to strive for spiritual understanding and then receive a confirmation, by the Spirit, that what he understood was correct. The writing was all in his own words, and yet a level of language came from him that was quite unexpected.

As Joseph did the translating, Emma became his first

Emma Hale Smith

scribe, writing the words he spoke. She had been a school-teacher and was a much better writer than Joseph. She was not allowed to look at the plates. However, on one occasion she lifted them up and felt the thin metal pages through the fabric wrapping Joseph kept around them.

Emma later described Joseph's way of working. She said that he would begin a new session without looking at the previous day's translation, or even so much as asking for any part to be reread, and yet he would continue with perfect consistency. He struggled with the language at times. He was not sure how to pronounce the name *Sariah*. On one occasion he came to a reference to the walls of Jerusalem. He stopped and asked, "Emma, did Jerusalem have walls surrounding it?" When she said it did, he replied, "Oh, I thought I was deceived."

Emma would later say, "Joseph Smith could neither write nor dictate a coherent and well-worded letter, let alone dictating a book like the Book of Mormon." Joseph was an unlearned farm boy, and yet what came from his lips

was an amazingly complex account of an ancient people on
the American continent. The text contained thousands of
names of places and people and covered centuries of time. It
was a book of scripture similar to the Bible in its prophecy
and divine message, even in its eloquence.

In February Martin Harris came to the Hale farm and
agreed to help with the writing, relieving Emma of that
duty. But Martin wanted proof that the Book of Mormon
was genuine. On one occasion he took a sample of the tran-
scribed characters to some language professors in New York
City for verification. He came back satisfied. Later he asked
if he could show the translation to his skeptical wife and a
few family members.

Joseph asked the Lord what he should do. Twice the
Lord revealed to Joseph that he must not allow Martin to
borrow the translated pages. But Martin was persistent.
After a third request, Joseph received a revelation that Martin Harris could take the papers and show them to certain
family members.

On June 14, 1828, Martin left for Palmyra with the 116
pages of the translated manuscript. The next day Emma
gave birth to a son, who lived only a few hours. Joseph
named the boy Alvin, in honor of his brother. For two
weeks Emma lay very ill. Gradually, as she began to improve, Joseph returned to practical matters. He began to
wonder what had happened to Martin and the pages of
manuscript.

Emma encouraged Joseph to hurry to Palmyra to see
what had happened. What followed was one of the darkest
periods of Joseph's life. He learned that Martin Harris had
broken his vow. He had showed the pages to many people
and then, somehow, he had lost them. Joseph suspected
Martin's wife of stealing them, but there was nothing to be
done. The pages were gone.

Joseph was greatly humbled. He had asked the Lord for this favor, and now it had turned into disaster. His first thought was to begin all over. However, Moroni appeared to him, scolded him, again forgave him, and then told him that he should not retranslate the opening section of the plates. Later Joseph learned, through revelation, that evil persons had the missing pages and could use them to claim there were discrepancies in the new translation. Joseph was told to translate another section of the plates, an account of the same time period but written by another ancient prophet.

Joseph returned to Harmony, where he would eventually be allowed to begin translating again. He faced a difficult winter, with scanty provisions and the disappointment of knowing his work had been slowed. But it was also a time of spiritual growth. He was often in contact with the Lord, receiving many revelations that he wrote down and that would become very important to those who would eventually accept him as a prophet. One promise he received from the Lord was that a new scribe would come to him, and it wasn't long before this prophecy was fulfilled.

A young man, a schoolteacher named Oliver Cowdery, had boarded with the Smith family in New York. After learning of Joseph's work, he decided to go to Harmony to meet him. Accompanied by Joseph's brother Samuel, Oliver walked the 125 miles on the muddy roads, often in rain. When he arrived at Harmony, he spent two full days in conversation with Joseph; then he began serving as the new scribe.

Joseph and Oliver found themselves constantly excited by the things they learned each day as Joseph translated. By May they had made a great deal of progress. One day they came to a passage that raised in their minds a question about authority. What person or persons on the earth had the au-

Joseph Smith and Oliver Cowdery translating the Book of Mormon

thority to administer the ordinances of the gospel? Who, for instance, had the power to baptize in Christ's name?

Joseph and Oliver were so disturbed by this question that they decided to go to a private place to pray about it. They went to a spot near the banks of the Susquehannah River. As they began to pray, a light suddenly shone above them and an angel appeared. Joseph had known such experiences before, but he had never shared such a moment with someone else. Now Oliver saw the glorious figure and heard him speak.

The angel told them that he was John the Baptist and that he had been sent by the ancient apostles Peter, James, and John. He laid his hands upon the heads of Joseph and Oliver and ordained them to the Aaronic Priesthood. This priesthood, he said, "holds the keys of the ministering of angels, and of the gospel of repentance, and of baptism by immersion for the remission of sins."

The angel told them that at a later time they would receive the higher, or Melchizedek, priesthood, which would give them the power to lay hands on others to give them the gift of the Holy Ghost. Joseph would, in time, become First Elder in a church that he would organize under divine direction, and Oliver would be Second Elder.

The two men, who now had the proper authority, then baptized each other and ordained each other to the Aaronic Priesthood, following the instructions of John the Baptist.

Sometime in May or June of that year, Joseph and Oliver were visited by Peter, James, and John, the ancient apostles. Once again hands were laid upon their heads, and this time the Priesthood of Melchizedek was restored, giving the two men the keys to begin the restoration of the Church of Jesus Christ on earth.

Their excitement in the work they were engaged in was even greater now, and they felt that they were learning more rapidly than ever before. But the skepticism of the Hale family and others in the neighborhood made Harmony a difficult place for them to work in. Preachers denounced Joseph from the pulpit, and neighbors began to harass him. There were even threats against his life.

Oliver Cowdery had a friend named David Whitmer, who lived in Fayette, New York. Oliver encouraged Joseph to contact him. In May 1829, David Whitmer invited Joseph and Oliver to come to his home. Many in the area had heard of Joseph's work and wanted to learn more about it. This was the atmosphere Joseph needed to continue the translation, so he agreed to go. Emma remained behind for a short time and then followed him to Fayette.

Peter and Mary Whitmer, David's parents, had seven children; three were married, and three sons and a daughter were still at home. It was to this farm home that Joseph was invited. The Whitmers, Pennsylvania Germans, were well-known and respected in their community, and they were deeply religious. As they became better acquainted with Joseph and heard his story, the Spirit bore witness to them that the work was of God.

Joseph now had a good setting for the translation, but the weather was hot, and he and Oliver worked very long hours. Sometimes Emma or one of the Whitmers took over the chore of scribe for a time, but Joseph stayed at the work without much rest.

Occasionally, the translation would not come to him. On one occasion he was distressed by something Emma had done. He went upstairs and tried to continue translating but was unsuccessful. He went into the woods to pray and was gone an hour. When he returned, he apologized to Emma and then went back to work—and the translation went well again. David Whitmer said, "He could do nothing save he was humble and faithful."

Many in the area around Fayette came to believe in Joseph Smith's calling. Some accepted that he had received authority from God and were baptized. But others doubted, including Martin Harris. The previous March, Joseph had been promised in a revelation that when the plates were finished, he would be allowed to show them to three witnesses. Martin came to Fayette and asked Joseph if he could be one of those witnesses.

As Joseph neared the completion of the translation, one day he urged Martin to repent and prepare himself to be a witness. He took Martin, Oliver Cowdery, and David Whitmer to the woods later that day, and they sat on a log and talked for a time. Then they knelt and all four prayed that they might see the plates, and each in turn prayed again. But nothing happened. Finally Martin stood up, said that it was his own lack of faith that was interfering, and withdrew from the others.

Shortly after that, a light appeared and an angel revealed

himself to Joseph, Oliver, and David. In front of the angel was a table, and on it were the plates, the breastplate and Urim and Thummim, and the sword of Laban, which was mentioned in the Book of Mormon. David Whitmer reported that the voice of God spoke to them, proclaiming the book to be true and translated correctly.

Joseph arose then and sought out Martin Harris, and the two prayed together. Again the vision opened, and Martin saw the angel and the other artifacts.

When the four men returned to the Whitmer home, Martin was overjoyed. At last his battles with doubt were over. "I have now seen an angel from heaven," he said, "who has of a surety testified of the truth of all that I have heard concerning the record, and my eyes have beheld him."

But it was Joseph Smith who was most relieved. He no longer had to bear witness alone. Others had seen the plates now and had received testimony from heavenly messengers. "I feel as if I was relieved of a burden which was almost too heavy for me to bear," he said, "and it rejoices my soul, that I am not any longer to be entirely alone in the world."

A few days later Joseph was allowed to share the burden with an even larger circle. The four Whitmer sons and a son-in-law, Hiram Page, along with Hyrum, Samuel, and Joseph Smith, Sr., all were allowed to see the plates. They walked into the woods, and there Joseph placed the plates in their hands and allowed them to touch the metal, turn the pages, and look upon the ancient characters.

The time was ready for the book to be published. When it was printed, it contained the testimony of Martin Harris, David Whitmer, and Oliver Cowdery, and another testimony by the eight additional witnesses. All said they had seen the plates, that they knew that they were real, and that Joseph Smith had translated them through divine power.

CHAPTER 4

The Church of Jesus Christ

The Book of Mormon was published in March 1830. Martin Harris mortgaged his farm to pay for the printing. With the book coming out, it was time for the creation of a formal church organization. On April 6, 1830, a group of believers—more than fifty in number—met in Fayette, New York, in the Whitmers' home. Most of those in attendance were members either of the Smith or Whitmer families. A church was legally organized under the name of the Church of Jesus Christ. (Through revelation, the name would be changed in 1838 to The Church of Jesus Christ of Latter-day Saints.)

Joseph Smith and Oliver Cowdery were ordained First Elder and Second Elder, while Hyrum and Samuel Smith and David Whitmer and Peter Whitmer, Jr., were also ordained to the office of elder. In addition, through revelation, Joseph was designated "a seer, a translator, a prophet, an apostle of Jesus Christ." He would serve as head of the Church, the only leader to act as the Prophet and to receive revelation for the Church.

Several persons in attendance were baptized that day. Joseph's greatest joy was to see his father baptized. Joseph

Smith, Sr., had steadfastly resisted joining any church. Now he accepted this new organization as the true church of Jesus Christ. The younger Joseph was so moved by his father's faith that he walked into the woods, out of the sight of others, and sobbed. Joseph Knight, Sr., Joseph's longtime friend, said that he never saw anyone so full of joy as Joseph was at that moment.

Such was the feeling among those who met that day. They were moved by the Spirit; they were filled with joy. And yet, what an overwhelming task they faced! They must take their message to the entire world. They were a mere handful of people living in a rural area. Most of them had very little education and few financial resources. And yet they viewed their task with optimism. If angels had appeared, if a prophet had been called, if God was working with them—anything could be accomplished.

But they were not angels themselves; they were human beings, with faults and frailties. They would make mistakes. The rise of the Church of Jesus Christ is a story of hard work, many defeats and disappointments—and steady growth. The work that the little group of believers began on April 6, 1830, succeeded beyond anything anyone outside the group could have expected.

The Church was founded on the basis that authority to act in Christ's name had been restored to the earth. What Joseph had been told many years before, at the time of his first vision, was that the churches that existed had strayed from the simple truths of Christ's gospel. The first missionaries of the newly restored church taught that the ancient church, through apostasy, had been lost from the earth. Now a church existed that possessed the ancient authority and was led by a prophet who was in contact with God, just as ancient prophets had been.

Many of the doctrines that would eventually govern the

Church had not yet been received. But as proof that the restoration of the gospel had begun, the missionaries carried with them the Book of Mormon. It was their witness that the "heavens were open" once again.

The most distinctive quality of the new church was the very method of obtaining doctrine: direct revelation from God. No longer was it necessary for preachers and theologians to interpret and debate the scriptures, which so often led to confusion and disagreement. Just before the organization of the Church, Joseph Smith received a revelation that would later be included as section 20 in the collection of revelations that would be called the Doctrine and Covenants. In that revelation, the basic principles of the gospel, the organization of the Church, and the duties of those who hold the priesthood were all explained by the Savior, Jesus Christ.

Most of those who accepted the message in those early years of the Church were converted by reading the Book of Mormon. As they read and followed the missionaries' advice to pray about the book, they became convinced that the translator must indeed be a prophet. When Jared Carter, one early convert, read the book, he prayed that the Lord would show him whether it was true. "I became immediately convinced that it was a revelation of God," he said.

The Church also rejected some of the doctrines common to most Christian churches, such as infant baptism, salvation through grace alone, and the "trinity" concept of the Godhead. The restored church taught that children should be baptized at the age when they become responsible for their own sins (later explained as age eight), that "good works" are an essential part of salvation, and that God, Jesus Christ, and the Holy Ghost are separate personages.

But if some persons accepted these teachings and became converted, most did not. Preaching the gospel of Jesus Christ was not unusual at that time. But these missionaries preached that an apostasy had occurred, that Christ's original church had been lost from the earth, and that this new church organization was the genuine Church of Christ restored, with authority to baptize. Many people were disturbed by such claims.

Before long the members of the Church were nicknamed "Mormons" because of their belief in the Book of Mormon. They gradually came to accept and to use that name. Latter-day Saints, LDS, and the Saints are other familiar short titles used to describe members of the Church. Joseph Smith explained that the name "Saint" did not mean that members had reached sainthood, but only that they were striving to serve the Lord.

After the organization of the Church, Joseph returned to his farm in Pennsylvania. Soon after, Emma was baptized, as were most members of the Knight family and some of their friends and relatives in nearby Colesville, New York. Eventually, about sixty members became a part of the Colesville branch.

Joseph, meanwhile, received a revelation that he should begin the work of translating the Bible through inspiration, to correct the translating mistakes in the King James Version. He also had to be concerned with making a living to care for his family on his little farm.

But this was difficult. Opposition to the Church was running high. Joseph was dragged into court on a charge of "disorderly conduct." His offense was preaching the Book of Mormon as true scripture. He did not deny the charge. But even though many hostile witnesses testified against him, he was acquitted. Almost immediately he was arrested again and threatened by an angry mob. Though he was acquitted a second time, the opposition was growing ugly. In Colesville, members of the Church were being harassed and vandalized. It was not safe for Joseph even to enter the town.

These cannot have been easy times for Emma. Joseph's

prospects for providing for his family were not good, because of his religious preoccupations. Added to this, she was pregant again. During this time Joseph received a revelation directed to her. In the revelation Emma was named an "elect lady," and she was called "to expound scriptures and to exhort the church," duties that were not normally expected of women at that time. She was also told to spend time writing and "learning much." Finally she was given the specific duty of gathering hymns for a church hymnal.

The revelation must have been a comfort to Emma; all the same, it was clear that she and Joseph could not stay in Pennsylvania. Since the strongest branch of the Church was in Fayette, as were most of the leaders, it seemed time for Joseph to move there, even though that meant giving up his farm.

During the summer of 1830, Joseph Smith, Sr., with his young son Don Carlos, went on a mission for the Church, as did Joseph's other brothers. Joseph, Sr., and Don Carlos visited relatives in St. Lawrence County, New York. Some were skeptical, but many more were interested, and eventually most of them accepted baptism.

Earlier, the Prophet's brother Samuel had been one of the first missionaries on behalf of the Church. He left a copy of the Book of Mormon with a Methodist minister and his wife, a couple named Greene. Samuel encouraged both to pray about the book, and within two weeks they became converted. Of special significance was that Samuel was introduced to one of Mrs. Greene's brothers, Phineas Young. And through that contact, eventually Phineas, Brigham, and Joseph Young, along with their friend Heber C. Kimball, all came into the Church. Brigham Young and Heber Kimball would later become two very important leaders of the Saints.

In fact, the early years of the Church turned out to be re-

Early missionaries

markable times for the numbers of leaders converted to the Church. For the most part, they were not people of great learning or wealth, but they were spiritual, loyal people who would lead the Church through very difficult times.

One such man was Parley P. Pratt. He felt compelled one day to leave his home in Ohio and to travel and teach the gospel as he understood it. He had been influenced by a group known as Campbellites, who believed that Christ's ancient church had been lost from the earth and needed to be restored. As he traveled by barge on the Erie Canal in up-state New York, he was suddenly moved upon to get off the boat, although he did not know why. On a chance encounter, he learned about the Book of Mormon. His interest was aroused, and he set out to find Joseph Smith. Instead, he met Hyrum Smith, the Prophet's brother. He and Hyrum sat up and talked all night, and then Parley read the Book of Mormon. He became convinced that the book was true and that the newly organized Church was indeed the beginning of the restoration he had hoped for. On September 1, 1830, he was baptized in Palmyra by Oliver Cowdery. Parley then visited his brother, Orson Pratt, in Canaan, New York, and told him about the Church. Soon Orson too was converted.

Soon after his conversion, Parley was called to go with three other missionaries to the western boundary of Missouri to preach the gospel to the Indians and to consider the area as a possible gathering place for the Church. Along the way, he and the missionaries stopped in Kirtland, Ohio, where many of the Campbellites lived. They were successful in converting Sidney Rigdon, a prominent Campbellite minister, who in turn helped to convert many in his congregation. About 130 persons from Kirtland and surrounding towns soon came into the Church.

When this news reached Joseph Smith, he became very excited. The growth of the Church was accelerating fast. And Sidney Rigdon, who soon came to visit Joseph, turned out to be a fine preacher, a learned man by the standards of the time, and a source of tremendous strength in the early years of the Church.

The question now became where the center of the Church should be, for Joseph had received a revelation that a gathering was to take place and that the Saints were to move to a central location to build up a society of faithful members. He was seriously considering western Missouri as the gathering site. For now, however, Kirtland seemed to offer a possible alternative. He asked the members in the branches in New York to gather to Ohio, and he would move there himself.

In early 1831, Joseph and Emma set out for Kirtland. Sidney Rigdon was with them in the sleigh, along with Edward Partridge, another new convert from Ohio. It was a bitterly cold winter, one of the coldest in American history, and the snow was very deep. The four travelers spent their nights in wayside inns or with farmers, and their days pushing through heavy snow. Their discomfort was great, especially Emma's, for her baby was due in April. But their anticipation of gathering with the Saints made them optimistic. Hundreds of faithful persons had joined the

Church already, including some who were proving to be excellent leaders. And Joseph continued to receive revelations from the Lord and to receive divine guidance in leading, teaching, and directing the affairs of the kingdom.

CHAPTER 5

Establishing Zion

Joseph and Emma arrived in Kirtland on February 1, 1831. Joseph jumped down from the sleigh and walked with confidence into the Gilbert and Whitney store. He threw out his hand to a man he had never seen before and said, "Newel K. Whitney! Thou art the man!"

Newel Whitney hardly knew what to think. "Stranger," he said, "you have the advantage of me. I could not call you by name, as you have me."

"I am Joseph the Prophet. You've prayed me here. Now what do you want of me?"

And so Joseph introduced himself to Kirtland, Ohio. His way of doing so says much about what was happening to him. He was becoming comfortable with the idea of being a prophet. His strength, his outgoing manner, his jovial good nature, and above all his trust in his spiritual gifts—all were coming together to make him a mature leader.

The fact was, Newel Whitney had been praying. He and his wife, Elizabeth Ann, had prayed for guidance, and they had heard a voice, which said to them, "Prepare to receive the word of the Lord, for it is coming." Shortly thereafter the Mormon missionaries arrived, and the Whitneys were converted. Joseph, meanwhile, had seen in vision Newel kneeling in prayer, so he recognized the man the moment he looked at him.

By now three hundred people in the vicinity of Kirtland had joined the Church. They were overjoyed to have the Prophet with them. The Whitneys took Joseph and Emma into their home, and there they stayed for several weeks.

During the following weeks many other Latter-day Saints were migrating toward Ohio. Sixty members from Colesville, New York, mostly relatives of the Knight family, traveled overland and by canal to Lake Erie, only to be delayed when the lake was frozen.

Another group from Fayette, New York, led by Lucy Smith, also made its way to Lake Erie, where they overtook the Colesville Saints. Joseph Smith, Sr., had gone ahead to Kirtland, but the Prophet's mother, never one to shy from a challenge, was a strong and able leader. She told her group to pray for the harbor to open. Soon after, the ice cracked, making a noise like "bursting thunder." The crack stayed open long enough for Lucy's chartered ship to slip through. Her group, as a result, arrived in Ohio well ahead of the Colesville members.

All through the spring and summer of 1831, new converts to the Church flowed into Kirtland. One man wrote: "They came, men, women and children, in every conceivable manner, some with horses, oxen, and vehicles rough and rude, while others had walked all or part of the distance. The future 'City of the Saints' appeared like one besieged. Every available house, shop, hut, or barn was filled to its utmost capacity. Even boxes were . . . used for shelter until something more permanent could be secured."

The new arrivals settled in Kirtland and a few surrounding towns in the part of Ohio called the Western Reserve. This section, in the northeast corner of the state, was once

owned by Connecticut. Much of the area was still covered
with dense forests.

In one sense, it was primitive country, with farmers still
clearing the forests and turning the soil. In another sense,
the connection to the East Coast was well established, with
the Great Lakes and the Erie Canal creating a direct tie for
traveling and shipping. In addition, many of the settlers
were New Englanders who brought their culture with them.
Most of them could read and write, and some were even
quite well educated.

Churches and schools were already established in the
new communities. Religious enthusiasm ran high in the area
around Kirtland, especially with so many Campbellites
there. Some of these people were open to Joseph's message.
The majority, however, did not accept the Church, did not
believe that Joseph Smith was a prophet. Anti-Mormon
feelings were extreme. Some local newspapers printed every
negative rumor about Mormons, never checking the
sources.

All the same, it was an exciting time for those who had
accepted the Church. It was also a time for learning new
doctrine and establishing a more complete organization.
Joseph received many revelations during his early months in
Ohio. These were often answers to specific questions, sometimes even advice to specific members who wanted to know
what their calling or mission was to be.

Meetings were quite different from what we see in modern churches. It was not uncommon for a church service—
often held out-of-doors—to last many hours, with very long
sermons. Children learned to be patient with the long meetings; most adults were much involved.

Joseph was becoming a good preacher by that time.
Several people recorded in their journals that they could
listen to him for as long as he chose to speak. His manner

was varied, full of humor and good-natured wit, yet power-ful. He loved to analyze and explain, "laying out the doc-trine" that he was receiving from God.

One of those doctrines he began to teach—a doctrine he had received by revelation—was that a special gathering place was to be built. The members would combine their forces in this place, called "Zion," and then from there the message of the restoration of Christ's gospel would be taken out to all the world. The Book of Mormon had spoken of a Zion on the American continent, a New Jerusalem, a city for a righteous people who would become a light unto the world.

Missionaries to Missouri reported that the area near In-dependence, Jackson County, was ideal for the building of Zion. The land was good and relatively cheap, and the population was sparse. It was a place where the Church would have room to establish itself and expand.

The dream of Zion was more than just a place to live with fellow believers; it was a place where all would prosper together by sharing resources. The law of consecration would be the governing principle. Each family would con-secrate, or give, all its worldly goods to the Church. In re-turn, the family would receive an inheritance, or steward-ship, according to their needs. This would usually take the form of land, which family members were to farm diligently. In return, they would receive the benefits of their own labor. But they were to retain only what they needed; the excess would be turned over to a bishop. These goods would be used to help poorer members until they could prosper by their own labors.

The Colesville Saints settled on land near Kirtland pro-vided by Leman Copley, a member of the Church, and they began the first attempt to live the law of consecration. Soon after, the Prophet received a revelation that they should be the first group to settle in Jackson County, Missouri. In June, Newel Knight led the Colesville branch to Independence. At the same time, twenty-eight elders were commanded to travel to the same destination, preaching along the way.

Then Joseph himself, along with several other Church leaders, began the trip to Missouri. Some of this group would stay there. Edward Partridge was called to serve as bishop, to administer the new law of consecration. William W. Phelps, a recent convert and experienced newspaper editor, was to open a printing business, while Sidney Gilbert would set up a store.

Joseph's party traveled by canal boat and stagecoach, and then by riverboat to St. Louis. From there they walked 240 miles, all the way across the state of Missouri.

In Independence, the men found the area to be beautiful, with rich land and green rolling hills. But to Joseph it seemed that he had gone back in time a hundred years. While there were educated people in the region, many who lived around Independence could not read or write, and they lived in crude conditions. Their homes were log cabins with no glass in the windows, the openings often covered with oiled animal skins. Hogs wallowed in the dooryard. The men and women dressed in skins, and children rarely wore shoes. A few log churches had been built, but the people were mainly trappers, hunters, and backwoods settlers from Kentucky or Tennessee. They took little interest in religion or in education. There were very few schools.

What Joseph saw, however, was the future and not the unimpressive present. He envisioned a temple on a hill, just outside Independence. He saw the whole region gradually filled with believing Saints, who would live in harmony. There would be no poor, because all would be given a chance to succeed. And there would be no rich, because the wealthier members would give of their excess for the sake of building up the kingdom of God.

In the next few days Church leaders dedicated a site for the temple and consecrated the region as Zion, the place for the gathering. The first log was laid for a church building, which would also serve as a school. Twelve elders, symbolizing the twelve tribes of Israel, set the log, and Joseph described his vision of what was to come.

The Colesville branch established itself in an area called Kaw Township, southwest of Independence. The settlement lay on the Big Blue River near the very heart of what is now Kansas City, Missouri. The next few months were not easy for the settlers. Few of them were farmers, and none had experienced such a primitive life. They took on a task that few on the great plains had tried: plowing through the prairie grass. It took eight or more oxen on a single plow just to turn over the deep sod.

The families camped as best they could in tents and shelters, and all gathered together to raise one house after another. Children worked very hard alongside the adults. Because they planted their crops late, the harvest was scanty. The winter was a very hard one, with the people living in crowded conditions, and they suffered a good deal from illness. But the Saints were single-minded in their goal. They had to survive and create a city—Zion. It was to be a light unto the world.

SECTION II

GATHERING TO ZION

During the rest of Joseph Smith's life, he would attempt to bring the members of the Church of Jesus Christ to a central gathering place: a city where the gospel could bring peace to the Saints. But Mormons were to have peace only in small portions. Attempts to gather together would lead to rejection by neighbors, harassment, and armed attacks.

The first years of the Church were filled with trials and pain—but trials have their value. Only the strong, the committed, would make it through the challenges, and their strength would be multiplied. The weak would be sifted out, and what would remain would be a sturdy base upon which the future could be built. Modern Mormons often look back to the early years of their church and find strength in the example.

CHAPTER 6

Attacks on the Prophet

Before Joseph Smith left for Missouri, he and Emma had moved into a one-room log cabin on the Morley farm near Kirtland. It was a humble home, especially since Joseph and Emma had left almost all their furniture and other possessions behind in New York. It was in this little cabin that Emma gave birth to twins, a boy and a girl, who lived only three hours.

Emma had endured much—the break with her family, the abandonment of their home in Pennsylvania, the difficult move to Ohio—but this new heartbreak was worst of all. Just one day later, however, Julia Murdock, a Mormon woman, died after giving birth to twins, a boy and a girl. John Murdock, the father, now had five children to raise by himself. He knew the twins could survive only if a woman could be found to nurse them. And so he turned to Joseph and Emma Smith, offering to let them adopt the twins.

Emma found comfort in the little babies, named Joseph and Julia. Soon after she took them in, Joseph departed for Missouri, and she spent the following weeks alone, caring for the newborn infants and accepting them as her own.

When Joseph returned to Kirtland, he continued to work on his translation of the Bible. He was not actually working from an ancient text; rather, he was making corrections through the power of revelation. Work was slow, however, because he was constantly visited by members of the Church seeking his counsel; by visitors seeking the truth; and sometimes merely by the curious, who wanted to see what manner of man he was.

On one occasion John and Elsa Johnson came to visit. They lived on a a farm near the settlement of Hiram, thirty-six miles south of Kirtland. As they sat with Joseph and Emma and a few others, someone asked whether God had given "any power to man" to heal the lame—as in the case of Elsa Johnson, whose arm was withered and useless.

Joseph walked over to Elsa, took her arm in his hands, and said, "Woman, in the name of the Lord Jesus Christ I command thee to be whole." Instantly, she could move her arm and even raise it above her head. The next day she washed clothes, working vigorously with the arm, and felt no pain. Her arm was healed.

John and Elsa Johnson were converted. But more than this, they invited Joseph to leave the little one-room cabin and to take up residence in rooms in their large farmhouse near Hiram. Such a move not only offered better living conditions for Emma and the twins but also offered Joseph the peace to work on the translation.

Joseph and Emma moved to the Johnson farm in September 1821. They had two rooms on either side of a large kitchen. Emma enjoyed the company of Elsa and the Johnson's daughter Nancy. She shared the chores of cooking and caring for the home, and she was happy for the pleasant surroundings for her babies.

The home also became headquarters for the operation of

the Church. Meetings with Church leaders were held there throughout the winter of 1831-32, and Joseph received some important revelations during this time.

It was in the Johnson home that Joseph and Sidney Rigdon received an important revelation about life after death. They testified that a vision opened before them, and they saw the glory of the Son, on the right hand of God, and witnessed the war in heaven and the defeat of Lucifer. Then they saw the "mansions" of heaven. Mankind will not be judged and sent either to heaven or hell, they learned, but will receive a just reward according to each individual's actions in this life. Most people will inherit one of three glories—the celestial, the terrestial, and the telestial—but the celestial glory places a person in the exalted state of living in the presence of God. This revelation was later included as section 76 of the Doctrine and Covenants.

In November a conference of Church leaders was held in Hiram. The men decided that it was time to publish Joseph's revelations in a work to be called the Book of Commandments. At this meeting a dispute began between Joseph Smith and William McLellin. William, along with a few others, felt that the language of the revelations should be improved and corrected. While Joseph did later make certain corrections in the language, the Lord was apparently not pleased with the attitude some of the men were taking toward the sacred writings. The Prophet received a revelation in which the brethren at the meeting were challenged to try their own ability at writing the words of God.

William McLellin was the only one willing to accept the challenge. But he failed miserably, finding that writing a revelation was not so simple as he thought. But then, he had watched Joseph, who made it seem easy. Parley Pratt once described the way Joseph received revelations: "Each sen-

tence was uttered slowly and very distinctly. . . . There was
never any hesitation, reviewing, or reading back, in order to
keep the run of the subject."

While William McLellin was satisfied, others were
not. If the winter seemed a tranquil one—a time for medi-
tation and writing—the quiet was somewhat deceptive. The
leaders of a growing opposition were Simonds Ryder and
Ezra Booth, both of whom had joined the Church and then
later turned against it.

Simonds Ryder was mentioned in one of Joseph Smith's
revelations, but when he received a copy, his name was
spelled "Rider." He interpreted this as meaning that the
Lord did not know how to spell his name. The spelling, of
course, was the fault of the scribe, who, like most people of
the time, spelled phonetically; it was not the fault of Joseph
Smith or the Lord. However, Ryder exaggerated the importance of the mistake and also objected to the law of consecration, as he understood it.

Ezra Booth found a number of complaints against the
Church. He believed that the Prophet was not as serious as
he ought to be, that he had a "spirit of lightness and levity,
and temper of mind easily irritated, and an habitual prone-
ness to jesting and joking." He also accused Joseph of in-
consistency and of false prophecies, and he objected to the
concept that only the Prophet could receive revelation for
the entire church.

Gradually, these two men became more open in their attacks. Ezra Booth published a series of unfavorable letters in
an Ohio newspaper, and he and Ryder spoke against Joseph
at every opportunity, stirring up bad feelings in the area
and giving ammunition to those who opposed the Church.
Finally, on March 24, 1832, after consuming a good deal
of whiskey, fifty men attacked Joseph Smith and Sidney
Rigdon.

Led by Simonds Ryder, the mob came at night, breaking into the Johnson house and dragging Joseph out of bed and outside. He was not easily taken, however. He fought to get one leg free, and used it to kick out at a man and knock him to the ground. The man, furious, grabbed Joseph by the neck and choked him until he was unconscious.

When Joseph regained consciousness, he was lying on the ground, with Sidney Rigdon nearby. Sidney had been dragged, and his head had bounced on the frozen ground. He was never the same after that night, his health and mind never quite as strong.

Joseph took Sidney for dead, and he asked the men to spare his own life. They responded by taunting him, telling him to call on his God to save him, and they threatened to mutilate his body. Then they carried him farther into a field and ripped off his clothes. One man cursed him and fell on him, scratching Joseph's body with his fingernails. "That's the way the Holy Ghost falls on folks," he yelled.

Tar was brought and smeared over Joseph's body. One of the men pushed the tar paddle into his mouth, and another

Joseph Smith tarred and feathered by a mob

forced a vial of poison between his lips. Joseph managed to resist, but the bottle broke one of his teeth. For years after, he spoke with a slight whistle.

Finally, the men rolled Joseph in feathers and left him lying unconscious on the ground. When he awoke, he cleared his mouth and nose of the tar and then managed to stagger back to his house. Emma had feared the worst as she had waited and tried to protect the twins, who were both sick with the measles; now when she saw Joseph in the dark, she thought the tar was blood, and she fainted.

During this time, John Johnson tried to escape his room, but the intruders held the door from the outside until he threatened to get his gun. Once free, he and his wife went to the aid of Joseph. They and other members of the Church spent the night applying lard to Joseph's body, trying to soften the tar so that it could be removed.

Though Joseph was exhausted and in great pain the next morning, Sunday, he preached a sermon from the porch of the Johnson home and didn't mention the attack upon him. Some of the men from the mob were even in the crowd. Later that day, moved by Joseph's bravery and spirit, three new members were baptized. Eventually, even some of the men involved in the attack joined the Church.

But the great sadness of that night turned out not to be the damage done to Joseph or even to Sidney Rigdon. Little Joseph, one of the adopted twins, was subjected to too much cold air. The child's illness grew worse and the following Friday he died.

Emma had given birth to three children, and all three had died. She had adopted two more, and now she had lost one of those. She and Joseph were heartbroken, but both were also resolved to carry out the work they had been called by the Lord to do. They looked ahead, not back.

CHAPTER 7

Troubles Brewing

Just three days after Joseph and Emma buried their little boy, Joseph left for Missouri a second time. He had planned to leave sooner but had delayed the trip because of the illness of the twins. He told Emma to take Julia to Kirtland, where the two of them would be safe.

Emma went to Kirtland expecting to stay with the Whitneys once again. Arrangements were supposed to have been made. Somehow, word never reached Elizabeth Whitney, and when Emma arrived, Elizabeth was sick in bed. An older aunt, who assumed much authority in the home, turned Emma away.

Emma was still suffering, and now she was reduced to searching out a place to live. She was soon shuttling about from one Mormon family to another. But she did not spend her time giving way to her grief. Lucy Smith, her mother-in-law, said that Emma was constantly finding ways to do service, helping and cheering those in need.

What Emma hadn't told anyone yet was that she was expecting another baby. This must have been a consolation to her, knowing that another child was coming, but it cannot have been an easy time. For one thing, she wondered whether her husband's life would ever be safe again, with such enemies about.

Joseph had these concerns and others. Not all was well in Jackson County, Missouri. Still, the accomplishments of the members had been remarkable. In less than a year, several settlements had been established, hundreds of acres of farm land had been opened, and dozens of homes had been built. Zion was taking shape. And most of the people had kept their commitment to the cause. Though they had little time for relaxation, the members were bound together by their shared purpose. Branches of the Church were growing, and meetings, often held in homes or out-of-doors, were intensely spiritual.

But Joseph also found that there were some problems in Zion, and not all were coming from outside the Church. Some members felt that others weren't working hard enough and weren't willing to sacrifice personal desires, as all had agreed to do. Edward Partridge tried to settle disputes and keep peace between the Saints, but some had grown bitter and left the Church.

The greatest complaint of the Missouri Saints, however, was that Joseph was continuing to stay in Ohio. Zion was in Jackson County. This was where the future lay, and the members felt that the Prophet should be there to direct the Church, to get them through these difficult early years.

Joseph met with the Saints, who welcomed him wholeheartedly, and he was able to relieve them of most of their concerns. Certainly he would be coming to Zion eventually, but the Lord had commanded him to stay in Ohio. For the present, that was still the headquarters of the Church. As usual, Joseph's love and enthusiasm were catching. The members were renewed by his strong but kindly sermons and private talks. By the time of his departure, they were in much better spirits.

But greater challenges lay ahead. The summer of 1832, after Joseph departed, circumstances got worse. New converts were moving into Jackson County almost daily, and the influx was difficult to handle. Those who arrived were often poor, placing a strain on the cooperative system. The work of plowing, planting, building log homes, and living in such primitive conditions was hard enough for these new settlers. But the crops turned out to be inadequate to feed all the new arrivals. The stress sometimes led to hard feelings and accusations between members again.

At the same time, complaints against the Church were being circulated among the old settlers in the area. They feared that the Mormons would eventually outnumber them and thereby take control. To the old settlers, Mormons were strange people. They talked about their religion constantly, and spoke of gifts of the Spirit, healings, and the like. Besides that, they befriended the Indians, whom settlers considered dangerous savages. The settlers, who had welcomed Mormons at first, were now beginning to stir up hostile feelings. In addition, the Saints often hurt themselves by responding with the claim that God had designated the land to them and would see to it that they someday possessed it all.

When Joseph left Jackson County, however, he was pleased with the progress of the members. He saw the challenges but trusted they could be handled. As he and his party returned to Ohio by stagecoach, an accident greatly delayed their arrival. Along the way, the horses suddenly bolted. Newel Whitney jumped from the stage and caught his leg in the spokes of the wheel, breaking bones in his foot and leg. Sidney Rigdon, who was with them, went on ahead to Kirtland, but Joseph stayed with Newel and nursed him back to health.

After four weeks, Joseph and Newel were finally able to

return home. But there was no going back to Hiram, where opposition to the Church was so violent. Joseph and Emma stayed with various families the rest of that summer until Joseph finally arranged to move into three storage rooms above the Gilbert and Whitney store. Not only did this provide adequate space for them, but Emma also sometimes took boarders into one of the rooms and thus added to their meager income.

Joseph and Emma had hardly moved in before Joseph was gone again. This time he went with Newel Whitney to New York City, where they arranged loans and bought merchandise for the Kirtland store, which Joseph was to run.

Joseph had never been to the big city of New York, and he was amazed at the modern buildings. While he found many of the people to be without religion and full of sin, he was impressed, as he wrote to Emma, that the Lord had created such "magnificent and splendid" things for mankind. The Lord was surely not displeased when people enjoyed the comfort of such blessings. He was only displeased with the misuse that people put them to. This attitude was to mark Joseph's thinking throughout his life. While many religious people of the time denounced all things worldly, he took joy in the pleasures that God granted to mankind.

The travelers arrived home in Kirtland on November 6, 1832, the same day that Emma gave birth to a baby son. Emma and her newborn son were both doing well. Joseph and Emma named the baby Joseph—later he was known as Joseph III—and his arrival brought great joy to them.

Joseph now set up shop in the store, continuing to spend his spare time working on his translation of the Bible. But his way of doing business was not very businesslike. He took pity on everyone who had a sad story to tell. He extended ~redit to many of his fellow Saints, and all too often they
¹ to make their payments. The store eventually sold out

of $20,000 worth of goods—but actually received very little of the money.

Though perhaps Joseph should have been more concerned, for the present he was very pleased with the state of things in Kirtland. For one thing, the Church was continuing to grow. Missionaries were being sent out constantly, and branches of the Church were being established all across the United States, especially in the northeast. Success was also being reported in upper Canada.

Leadership was also coming into the Church. One day when Joseph was chopping wood behind the store, three men approached him and identified themselves as Joseph and Brigham Young and Heber C. Kimball, all converts to the Church.

The three newcomers must have wondered about a prophet of God chopping wood in his shirt-sleeves, since men of stature didn't usually do such things, nor did they dress that way. But then, Heber Kimball and the Young brothers were practical, hard-working people themselves, and they were impressed by Joseph's down-to-earth manner. They were destined to be important figures in leading the Church and preaching the gospel in many parts of the world. Others may not have realized the importance of these converts, but Joseph seemed to know it from the beginning. He especially took to Brigham Young—a man of spirit and a man of action.

Brigham Young's wife Miriam had died, leaving him with two young daughters. He was a tradesman, a builder, a furniture maker, and, in that sense, a practical man. But he was also a man devoted to the gospel. He had already served a mission before coming to Kirtland to meet the Prophet.

During the first week that Brigham was in Kirtland, he spoke in tongues at a meeting of the Saints. Some were not sure how Joseph would react, but the Prophet said that the experience was of God and that Brigham had spoken in the pure language of Adam.

During the time the Smith family lived upstairs in the store, Joseph received several revelations. Some of them were answers to specific questions about the scriptures, about specific doctrines, about Church organizational matters, and about the problems developing in Missouri. In one revelation (section 87 in the Doctrine and Covenants) Joseph received from the Lord a specific prophecy that a great civil war would take place in the United States. This revelation was given three decades before the Civil War broke out, but the details of how it would happen were all correct. Another revelation (section 89) advised the Saints on how to keep their bodies healthy and strong. The Lord, through the Prophet, recommended a wholesome diet, stressing grains and fruits and some meat, but he warned against alcohol, tobacco, and hot drinks (later interpreted as meaning coffee and tea). This doctrine, known as the Word of Wisdom, gradually became the standard Mormons lived by.

Though many good things were happening in Kirtland, there were problems as well. Simonds Ryder and Ezra Booth were not the only opponents of the Church. A man named Doctor Philastus Hurlbut (Doctor was his given name), who had joined the Church and then been excommunicated for immoral behavior, became a bitter enemy. With the support of some other opponents, he traveled to Manchester and Palmyra, New York, and collected everything negative he could get anyone to say about Joseph Smith. These accounts were published by E. D. Howe.

Later studies showed that the New York neighbors of the Smiths were not nearly so ill disposed toward Joseph as ᵗʰ̵ut made them sound. Quite clearly, he led people to ᵉ negative statements. Nonetheless, the publication of his collection of denouncements struck a hard blow at Joseph. The statements were quoted in almost every book or article written about Joseph or Mormonism for several generations to come. Those who wanted to believe the worst about Joseph were only too pleased to have such a resource.

CHAPTER 8

The Loss of Zion

In Missouri, problems for the Saints continued to get worse. The old settlers, stirred up by local ministers and by community leaders, were becoming open in their hostility. Verbal attacks turned to harassment. Windows were broken, shots were fired, and cows were run off or killed.

Emily Partridge, just nine years old in 1833, was awakened one night by the tremendous blaze of a burning haystack near the house. Years later, she still remembered the terror of hearing men shouting, threatening, and vandalizing homes. Her little sister would wake up in the night and scream, "The mob are coming, the mob are coming."

Emily had already faced her share of challenges. When Bishop Partridge, her father, had been called to Zion, he left his family behind in Ohio. When they later followed him to Independence, their riverboat had been stalled by ice floe and they had been forced to stay in the little settlement of Arrow Rock for a few weeks. The Morley family was with them, and all fifteen persons had to make themselves "quite comfortable" in a little one-room log cabin.

Finally arriving in Independence, Emily discovered a very different world from what she had known before.

Women walked around barefoot, carrying heavy burdens on their heads. Families lived on corn bread, bacon, and coffee, and little else. Indians often passed through the town, and for an Eastern girl who had heard of Indian attacks, this was no easy adjustment.

Bishop Partridge moved his family into a log cabin. But even with so little space, Emily said, "Father being bishop he had to provide for the poor, and he took a widow with four children into the one room that we had, making fourteen or fifteen in the family."

But Emily also remembered happy times. Her father soon built a log house with one room on the first floor and one upstairs, and a cellar besides. She loved the dense woods, where plenty of nuts and berries grew for the gathering, and the vines that hung from the trees made perfect swings. Children attended school for only a few months of the year, but Emily was happy to have a school she could attend.

Her second year in Independence, however, turned into a year of terror. In July 1833, the hostility of the old Missouri settlers suddenly intensified. W. W. Phelps wrote an editorial that the old settlers interpreted as encouragement for freed slaves to move to Jackson County. While few people in the county owned slaves, most favored slavery and hated "abolitionists." The Mormons made no issue of slavery, but most of them were northerners and were opposed to the practice.

A great outcry over Brother Phelps's article was followed by all sorts of rumors. An extra edition of *The Morning and the Evening Star* was published to correct the false impressions of the article, but it was ignored.

The complaints against the Mormons were not surprising, given the differences between the two cultures. Old settlers considered Indians savages, while Mormons tried to

befriend them. The Prophet told the Saints to try to live in
peace with non-Mormons, but the older settlers feared that
the Mormons might try to take their land as a God-ordained
right.

Such a possibility did not seem remote to Missourians.
After all, Mormons lived in ways that the old settlers didn't
understand. They combined all their holdings and shared
their harvests, and they claimed to heal the sick, to speak in
tongues, and to receive revelations.

In any case, the Mormons were gradually taking over the
area by sheer force of numbers. The old settlers, who had
prized the open country, saw the land being "filled up." How
long before the Mormons voted in all their own public officials and thereby controlled the whole county? If the old
settlers were willing to accept any rumor that spread through
the area, the Saints were not without blame either. Some of
them made things worse by bragging that God would soon
prepare a way to establish their city of Zion.

On July 20, 1833, a large crowd of old settlers gathered
in Independence. They wrote up and delivered a demand
that no more Mormons migrate to Jackson County and that
those who were there must sell their lands and move away.

When the Mormon leaders received this threat, they
were given no time to consider, and so they responded as
only they could. They said they would not accept the terms
of the proposal—the old settlers had no right to force them
to leave. When this reply came back to the people gathered
at the town square, they suddenly turned into a mob.

The mob moved just south of the town square to the
Mormon printing company. There they forced Sister Phelps
and her children out of their upstairs living quarters, de-
molished the press, and then pulled the building apart. The
sheets of the Book of Commandments, the collection of
Joseph Smith's revelations, were thrown into the street.

Attack on the first Latter-day Saint settlement in Missouri

Some of these sheets were saved by two young Mormon girls, who gathered them up and ran to hide in a cornfield.

The mob then went to Sidney Gilbert's store, where they tore things up and dragged goods into the street. From there they turned toward Bishop Partridge's house, a half mile out of town. On the way, they tore up a Mormon blacksmith shop and whipped some Mormon men.

Emily Partridge and her sister Harriet were returning from a spring with fresh water when they saw the mob gathering around their house. They waited in terror until the mob moved back toward town. The mob had taken their father, and Sister Partridge was despairing for his life.

Bishop Partridge, along with a young man named Charles Allen, was marched to the town square. Leaders of the mob demanded that they denounce the Book of Mormon or promise to leave the county. They refused to do either. Bishop Partridge told them he was willing to suffer for the sake of Christ, but he was not willing to leave.

Men grabbed him and began to strip his clothes off. Something about his submissive meekness, however, seemed to calm the crowd. They stripped him only to the waist and covered him with tar and feathers, but as he stood there, tall and erect, accepting their treatment, some of them lost their taste for what they were doing. One man threatened to whip him, but another said, "You have done enough."

Emily was watching out the upstairs window at home when she spotted two riders drawing close. She was terrified when she thought one of them was an Indian. Then she realized it was her father, covered with tar and feathers. The family and other friends helped clean him up, but acid had been added to the tar, and his body was badly burned.

Three days later, the mob returned, riding through the settlement with a red flag symbolizing blood. This time they forced a number of the Mormon leaders to the public square and demanded that they leave the county in two groups. The first must be gone before January 1, 1834, and the second by April. Given no options, and with no time to consult with the Prophet, the men were forced to sign the agreement.

The agreement put an end to harassment by the mob for the present, but the Saints were not convinced that they must adhere to an agreement forced on them by violence. They soon made contact with Joseph Smith, and he advised them to seek help through legal avenues but not to begin leaving the county.

The Saints sought help from Governor Daniel Dunklin, and at first he seemed to sympathize with them. He advised them, as Joseph Smith had done, to use the courts as a peaceful way of protecting themselves. The Saints therefore hired the legal firm of Alexander Doniphan to represent them.

But news soon spread that Mormons were arming themselves and planning to stay. On October 31, the violence started again. One after another of the settlements was attacked. Men were beaten, houses were torn down, and women and children were forced out into the cold.

Mormon men prepared to defend themselves, and shooting actually broke out in the Whitmer settlement, where two old settlers and one Mormon were killed. Philo Dibble was shot in the abdomen and given up for dead, but after a priesthood blessing, he recovered. A few days later he actually walked from the county under his own power.

At this point, the Mormons gathered a little army of about one hundred men. They met an armed "militia" of Missourians under the guidance of Thomas Pitcher, who demanded that they give up their weapons. Lieutenant Governor Lilburn Boggs then appeared and promised the Mormons that if both sides would give up their guns, negotiations would follow.

The Saints agreed and gave up their weapons, but Thomas Pitcher failed to disarm the old settlers. Once the Mormons were without means of self-protection, the old settlers set upon the various settlements, whipping and beating people and forcing them from their homes without even time to gather up a few belongings.

People in one settlement, forced to leave in great haste, headed south over the prairie. The first snows had come, and many of the children had no shoes. Under the snow were clumps of burned-off prairie grass, so sharp that it cut the children's feet. They left a trail of blood that others later found and followed. They were saved by good people in a neighboring county, who took pity on them.

Most of the Saints headed north to the Missouri River. A huge encampment gathered there and waited until ferries could take them across to Clay County.

A torrential rain had begun to fall. The misery of the Saints was terrible: the cold, the wet, the loss of belongings, injuries and illness. But the pain ran deeper. Zion had been lost. God seemed to have forgotten the Saints in their time of need, and an evil enemy had been allowed to triumph.

Though some of the Mormons gave up at this point and left to return to the East, most were resolute. Over the next few days, they managed to find temporary homes and shelters. Many people in Clay County were outraged by the behavior of those in Jackson County, and they opened up their homes, sheds, and barns to the Saints and offered them food and work. Some Mormons died from exposure and sickness that winter, but most managed to survive.

The Partridge family and the John Corrill family moved into a one-room stable. Once again, there were fifteen in a single room. They hung up blankets around a large fireplace and gathered in around the fire, since the rest of the room was bitterly cold. Even with the fire, however, the ink would freeze in the inkwell as Bishop Partridge tried to carry out his correspondence.

On November 13, something strange began to happen. That night a storm of meteors showered through the skies, as people throughout the land stood in awe and watched. Emily Partridge, like many another child, stood shivering in the dark and watched the meteor show. The children listened as they heard their parents try to explain what was happening. To many, it was a sign of God's majesty, proof that he was watching over them and that somehow all would be well.

CHAPTER 9

Zion's Camp

Joseph Smith watched the same meteor shower in Kirtland, and he too was impressed with the power of God. But it would be almost another month before he would hear of the trials of the Saints in Zion. Joseph, who was about to turn twenty-eight, had learned much. Now he faced a new burden. His people were dying for the sake of the gospel. The enemy had truly bared its teeth—and he was a thousand miles away, momentarily powerless to do anything to help.

In February 1834, Parley P. Pratt and Lyman Wight arrived from Missouri. They told Joseph that Governor Dunklin had agreed to help the Saints return to their homes, but only on the condition that the Mormons raise their own militia to protect themselves there. Joseph prayed about the problem and received a revelation that an army should be raised.

After two months of recruiting, fewer than two hundred men had volunteered to go to Missouri. Money for equipment and supplies was also hard to come by. The Saints in Kirtland and throughout the East were able to raise less than five hundred dollars. In May, the first group left Kirtland, planning to meet another group traveling from Pontiac,

Zion's Camp

Michigan. The combined militia group, under the leadership of Joseph Smith, would be known as Zion's Camp.
Eventually the camp was comprised of 205 men, 11 women,
and some children. They had twenty-five baggage wagons
stocked mostly with supplies for the Missouri Saints. The
men carried their own provisions on their backs, and they
walked—a march of almost a thousand miles.

George Albert Smith and Jesse Smith, cousins of the
Prophet, both went along. At sixteen, George Albert was
the youngest soldier. Joseph kept him close by and watched
out for him. Since George Albert kept a detailed journal,
much of what is now known about Zion's Camp came from
him.

George Albert was anything but a robust soldier. Tall
and awkward, he suffered from poor eyesight. The poverty of
many of the recruits was obvious in their dress, but perhaps
nowhere more so than in George Albert Smith. His trou-
sers—known as pantaloons—were made of striped cloth
normally used to make feather beds. His mother packed him
a knapsack made of checked apron fabric, and his father

gave him a new pair of boots. He wore a straw hat and car-ried an old musket, a relic of the Revolutionary War.

By the end of the first day, George Albert's feet were bloody and sore, and his pantaloons were ripped in shreds. He had sat on his straw hat and smashed it. With his red, squinty eyes, he must have seemed a pitiful warrior. But he was not alone; few of the men had suitable clothes and weapons. And everyone had sore feet.

The Prophet fared somewhat better. He had a handsome pair of horse pistols, a sword, and a rifle. But his feet were just as bloody as the rest. Boots at that time were not care-fully constructed to the shape of the foot. Joseph Young, one of the marchers, said that the soldiers walked until "the blood could be heard in our boots and shoes."

The army was organized in companies of twelve, each with a captain. Every person had a specific work assignment. They marched each day from twenty-five to forty miles. Then they had to make camp, with water to be carried in, meals prepared, and livestock fed. Brigham Young said that after walking all day and pulling baggage wagons through mud holes, he seldom got to bed until eleven or twelve. A horn to wake the men was sounded long before sunup, but, wrote George Albert Smith, "There was scarcely a night that we could sleep, for the air rose from the ground hot enough to suffocate us, and they supplied musketos in that country, as they did eggs, by the bushel."

The food was not bad at first, but it got worse as the men reached the open prairies. They lived on fried bread or corn dodgers (fried cornmeal mush), and they sometimes had to drink stagnant water. George Albert told of drinking water filled with "living creatures." He said he learned to strain the "wigglers" with his teeth as he drank.

The men did all they could to disguise their identity, but the appearance of such a large group raised many questions.

Because of George Albert Smith's youthful appearance, he was chosen to respond to the curious. He had an artful way of seeming to answer questions without giving any real information. When asked where the group was from, he would reply, "From every place but this, and we will soon be from this." And as to where they were going: "To the West."

The men were dedicated to their purpose, some even excited about the possibility of fighting for their brothers and sisters in the gospel. But that did not make the daily drudgery any easier, and before long the complaints and even bitter accusations began. Finally the Prophet warned them that unless they repented and changed their spirit, a scourge would come upon them.

By the time the camp reached Missouri, word had reached Jackson County that an army was coming to destroy all the old settlers. The numbers of Mormons in the army was greatly exaggerated, and there were rumors that Indians would fight with them. Panic spread among the Missourians, and war seemed imminent.

Joseph made several attempts to head off trouble. He sent messengers ahead to Jefferson City to meet with the governor. But by now Governor Dunklin was singing quite a different tune from the one the Mormons had heard earlier. Afraid of civil war, he withdrew his offer to provide a military escort for the Saints to return to their homes.

As Joseph and his small army continued to march toward their fellow Saints in Clay County, the purpose of their march was becoming lost. It did not appear likely that two hundred men could take on the thousands of old settlers in western Missouri. At a meeting in Liberty, Missouri, representatives of the Missourians told the Mormons they could not live in the same county with them, but they were willing to buy all Mormon-owned lands for double value, and to pay within thirty days. The Mormons had to promise, however, never to return. As an alternative, the Mormons could buy out the old settlers on the same terms.

Double value may have seemed a handsome offer, but the old settlers knew what they were doing. The Saints could never promise not to return. To them, Jackson County was Zion. Besides, mobs had plundered and stolen virtually all the improvements and belongings on those lands, and no offer was made to compensate for that. The old settlers also knew that the Mormons could never raise the money to buy them out.

The Saints in Clay County were frustrated, but they agreed to talk with Joseph Smith about the offer, and they promised that Zion's Camp would not enter Jackson County. Some of the Jackson County men, not willing to continue negotiations, prepared to return across the Missouri. One of them, James Campbell, vowed that eagles and turkey buzzards would eat his flesh within two days if he did not fix Joseph Smith's army so that their "skins will not hold shucks." In crossing the river, the boat capsized and all were swept into the water. Campbell was not found for three weeks, but eventually his skeleton was found in a pile of driftwood. His bones had been picked by birds. Accusations and rumors spread quickly that Mormons had drilled holes in the boat to make it go down.

On June 19, Joseph's little company began setting up camp between the two forks of Fishing River, just inside Clay County. Suddenly five men rode into camp on horseback and reported that an attack was coming that night, with men coming from Jackson County and other places.

As evening came on, dark clouds gathered. And then a storm broke out, the likes of which the men in Zion's Camp had never seen before. Lightning flashed and thunder rolled without interruption, as the rain fell in torrents. The men of the camp took refuge in a nearby country church.

Their attackers were not so fortunate. About two hundred planned to cross the Missouri, but the storm came up as the first group of about forty was crossing. The boat made it to shore but the men were beaten by enormous hailstones. They hid under wagons or wherever they could, while the hail broke limbs from trees around them and drove their horses away. By morning, they headed for home, defeated. One of the men said that if God always fought for the Mormons that way, there would be no conquering them.

During the next few days Joseph Smith was able to convince Clay County officials that he had not come to shed blood, but to seek justice for his people and to give them aid. He made a counteroffer to the old settlers to buy up their lands for a fair price, provided that the losses of the Saints would be deducted from the cost. He promised that the Saints would pay within a year and would stay out of the county until the old settlers had their money. The Missourians replied that they would not accept such a proposal.

That same day Joseph received a revelation (Doctrine and Covenants, section 105), which he announced to the men in Zion's Camp. The Lord had told him that the time had not yet come for the redemption of Zion. The faith of the Saints had been tried, but they were not yet worthy, for they had not learned to share with the poor and afflicted and had not yet become united. The Saints would return to their Zion only when they were prepared to live by celestial laws. In the meantime, those who were righteous would receive an endowment, or a special blessing to be granted in the temple that the Lord had commanded to be built in Kirtland.

For some of the men, this pronouncement was a bitter disappointment. They had expected to march into Zion and claim what was rightfully theirs. They expected God to march with them. Those who had opposed Joseph in the past were now especially bitter, and a few left the Church. Some of the men drew their swords and took out their anger on a patch of brush, mowing it down.

Joseph accepted the Lord's will, but he was also deeply disappointed. The perfect society he had envisioned in Jackson County would not yet be established; and, worse, many of his followers were accusing him of false prophecy and of leading them on a fruitless march of a thousand miles.

And then the scourge Joseph had predicted hit the camp. Cholera had been rampant along the Mississippi and Missouri rivers, and now it struck three members of Zion's Camp in one day. Within a few days the dreaded disease was raging through the entire group. Men fell sick suddenly and violently, and became delirious with fever. When Joseph tried to heal them, he was powerless; then he fell sick himself. Sixty-eight were stricken, and fourteen died. Among the dead was Betsy Parrish, who had traveled with the camp. Some of the Saints in Missouri also contracted the disease and died, including Sidney Gilbert, who had lost his store in Independence.

One of those who died was Joseph's cousin Jesse. He had joined the Church without the support of his father, and Joseph felt a special responsibility for him. This loss, combined with all the others, was a heavy burden for the Prophet.

George Albert Smith was also deeply grieved. He told Joseph that it would have been much better had he died, since he was not the man that Jesse was and would never serve the Church so well. Joseph reassured George Albert, telling him that he had no way of knowing the Lord's will in such things.

On July 2, Joseph Smith was inspired to tell the brethren of Zion's Camp that if they would now repent and promise to keep their covenants with the Lord, the plague would be stopped. The men raised their arms and made a covenant with the Lord. Cholera struck no one else after that.

Zion's Camp was disbanded. Each man was given his share of the remaining money, amounting to $1.14 each, and the men were instructed to make their own way home. Some decided to stay in Missouri, but most returned to their families in the East.

Joseph stayed for a time, helping to organize the Saints in Clay County and setting up a high council to aid Bishop Partridge in leading the Church. He left with sixteen others on July 9, traveling much of the way on foot, and arrived home August 1. By that time newspaper reports had reached the Saints in Ohio that the Prophet had been killed in Missouri, and Emma was left believing for a time that she had lost her husband.

In the Zion's Camp experience, Joseph had been through one of the greatest trials of his life, but he had also learned a great deal about leadership. George Albert Smith said that throughout all the ordeals, Joseph was patient, humble, and willing to do much more than his share. And even when he was fired to anger on occasion, he showed remarkable restraint.

Perhaps just as important was the fact that many others received valuable leadership training. Brigham Young later said that he wouldn't trade all the wealth in the county for what he had learned through his experience with Zion's Camp. Nine of the members of the first Quorum of Twelve Apostles and all of the members of the First Quorum of Seventies, organized soon after the march, were members of Zion's Camp. They were loyal and stalwart men who used the experience to gain strength. Those who passed the test went on to direct the affairs of the Church for the next generation.

And young George Albert Smith, the big, awkward boy

with the failing eyesight, not only kept the best written record of the excursion, but also went on to be an apostle at a very young age. He would eventually serve with Brigham Young in the First Presidency of the Church. He had learned much by being so close to Joseph Smith; he had received an incomparable schooling for his own future.

CHAPTER 10

Problems in Kirtland

During the winter of 1834–35, Joseph Smith took important steps to strengthen the Church. Earlier a First Presidency had been formed to lead the Church, with Joseph Smith as President and Sidney Rigdon and Frederick G. Williams as Counselors to the President. Joseph had now learned through revelation that twelve apostles were to be called, and that the three witnesses to the Book of Mormon would assist the Presidency in choosing that first Quorum of Twelve Apostles. Joseph's father was called as Patriarch to the Church, with the duty of giving special blessings to the membership.

The men called to be apostles were expected to travel throughout the world, to teach the gospel, and to help direct the affairs of the Church. The next spring they began their first missions in the eastern states. They traveled without "purse or scrip," which is to say, without money. They had to rely on the goodness of both members and nonmembers for their board and room, which often meant approaching a house, proclaiming oneself a minister of the gospel, and then asking for a place to sleep. This was a common practice in the nineteenth century, but it was not an easy way to live.

Nights spent out in the open, without supper, were not un-common.

Some men went on many missions. Erastus Snow, who didn't marry until somewhat late in life, only rarely returned from the mission field. Parley Pratt left his wife and children many times to serve missions. His missions were a series of amazing adventures. He was abused and jailed, threatened and chased. But he, and the other missionaries, met with great success, and many new converts continued to come into the Church. Many gathered to Kirtland, where there would eventually be about two thousand members.

Joseph Smith also traveled as a missionary. This, com-bined with some business trips to the East, meant that Emma was often left alone to look after the children, the home, and Joseph's business affairs. But she was a strong person, with good business sense, and she handled these separations well. In July 1836 she would give birth to another son, Fred-erick.

The Lord had promised at the time of Zion's Camp that the Saints would soon receive an endowment, or special blessing. As early as 1832 Joseph had received a revelation that a special house of worship, a temple, should be built. Later, he learned that it would have a meeting area on the first floor and room for a school on the second floor. The cor-nerstone was set in July 1833, and work proceeded on the building through the next three years.

At the same time, Joseph set about to improve himself and the other leaders of the Church. In 1833 he established a school for Church officers, the School of the Prophets. Theological subjects were taught, as well as practical lessons in nonreligious subjects. After the interruption caused by Zion's Camp, the school reopened with a somewhat differ-ent format. It was divided into the Elder's School, for reli-gious training, and the Kirtland School, for adult education in nonreligious areas. A teacher was hired to teach a course in Hebrew during the fall of 1835, and Joseph Smith was one of his students.

In the summer of 1835, a man named Michael Chandler brought some Egyptian mummies and manuscripts to Kirtland. Members of the Church eventually purchased these and presented them to the Prophet, and he began to translate the papers. Through inspiration, he produced an account of the ancient prophet Abraham. This account, titled the Book of Abraham, would become part of a collection of writings known as the Pearl of Great Price. In 1835, 101 of Joseph's revelations were also published as the Doctrine and Covenants.

Gradually life improved for the Saints in Kirtland. By the winter of 1835–36, many of the members had established homes and farms and were living quite comfortably. Prices had risen greatly, which caused hardship for new arrivals but also stimulated business and provided good returns for crops and various handcrafted goods.

The temple, which was nearing completion, was a beautiful structure. It stood on a hill overlooking the community, a symbol of the establishment of the Church as solid and lasting. Many of the women contributed their best china to be ground up into the plaster applied to the outside walls. The bits of china made the building shine beautifully in the sun. On the inside, ornately designed and crafted woodwork reflected the love and devotion of a people willing to sacrifice for a temple dedicated to the Lord.

All that winter, as the time for the temple dedication approached, the Saints seemed to grow in spirit. They felt the joy of prosperity, and above that the joy of living the gospel. Church meetings were moved into the temple as its completion drew near. Marriages were performed, and members gathered during the week for prayer meetings.

Kirtland

From January through May, a great series of heavenly visitations occurred at the temple. On January 21, Church leaders gathered in the nearly completed building for a new ordinance—the washing and anointing of God's chosen servants. That night Joseph saw a remarkable vision of the celestial kingdom of God. And there he saw his brother Alvin. He learned that the dead could have an opportunity to enter God's kingdom and continue to progress and learn after this life. Those who died without baptism could receive that blessing through special baptisms performed in the temple by the living on behalf of the dead.

For the dedication on March 27, members came from Missouri and from the East, along with all the Saints in the Kirtland area. Only a thousand people could get inside. Many others gathered at the doors and windows, and finally others met in a nearby log church.

The dedicatory services lasted seven hours that day. A long sermon was given by Sidney Rigdon—one of the greatest of his life. He thanked the people for their commitment and sacrifice to make the building possible. Joseph Smith delivered the dedicatory prayer (see Doctrine and Covenants, section 109). Hymns were sung, including a new one written for the occasion by William W. Phelps: "The Spirit of God Like a Fire Is Burning." Testimonies were borne, and during the meeting a number of spiritual manifestations took place.

Many in attendance bore witness that they had seen heavenly visitors. During the opening prayer a "glorious sensation" passed through the congregation, elevating the souls of all who felt it. Joseph Smith informed the audience that the apostle Peter had entered the temple and declared his acceptance of the dedication. Heber C. Kimball testified he too saw Peter, and he described his appearance. A choir of angels sang, and many recorded in their journals that they heard the music. At one point the sound of rushing wind was heard. Some who could not attend the meeting actually heard the wind and ran from their houses to see what it was. But the natural wind was not blowing; this was the wind of the Spirit, rushing into the building.

A week later, during Sunday services, Joseph Smith and Oliver Cowdery went behind the curtains of the temple and received a series of visions and visitations. Jesus appeared to them and pronounced the temple acceptable. Moses appeared and returned the keys for the gathering of the tribes of Israel. Elias and Elijah appeared, granting keys for the function of the priesthood, opening the way for the second coming of Christ.

On April 6, the apostles met all night in the temple, and they experienced the gift of tongues and visions of heavenly visitors.

Perhaps the time was too wonderful to last very long, but no one could have guessed how completely times would change over the next few months. Building the temple had not only created a spirit of cooperation and devotion, it had also stimulated business by creating jobs and adding money to the economy in Kirtland. Prices for land rose quickly because of the arrival of so many new residents. This land value gave people something to borrow money against, and many began to go into debt and live much better than they ever had before. The Mormons were not alone in this; the whole nation was riding on an economic boom that was based mainly on optimistic speculation.

With the growth, Kirtland needed a more solid economic base. A bank was needed to provide investment money to support businesses. Currency was also needed as a means of exchange, since most of the wealth of the area was in land, which was not an item of exchange.

The Prophet, after conferring with other Church leaders, decided to open a bank. He sent to the East for plates to print money (banks printed their own in those days), and at the same time he applied for a bank charter. The state, however, refused to approve a new bank in Kirtland. State banking executives had recently become more conservative about the spread of banks and were denying most applications.

Joseph was in a dilemma. He had ordered the expensive plates, and he knew that a bank was needed. A "joint stock" company was legal without a charter, so he decided to start a company that would function as a bank but not be called one. In order to use the printing plates, he had the letters "anti-" added in front of the word "bank" and "ing" attached behind, so that the paper was printed with the words "Kirtland Safety Society *anti-banking* Company."

While the company possessed some gold and silver coin to back the paper money, most of its worth was in land. This created doubt in many minds about reliability, as did the fact that the organization had no charter from the state. The bank therefore got off to a bad start.

Church leaders had relied on the trust that the economy would continue to go well. In 1837, the entire nation went into an economic panic. Banks began to fail. In Kirtland, many were out of work because the temple had been completed, and as businesses began to falter, rumors spread that the bank was failing. This caused a rush, with people demanding their money in gold and silver coin instead of paper currency.

Joseph tried desperately to keep the bank operating, but eventually he was forced to withdraw from its operation. Finally the doors of the bank had to be closed, with many people losing money.

As a result of the bank failure, much bitterness was directed toward the Prophet. In the minds of some people, a prophet should know everything and should never make a bad decision. Others recognized that the Prophet was not instructed in all things, and that the bank had been a reasonable decision but one that was doomed by the change in the economy and by certain events in Kirtland. All the same, bitterness was deep, usually with those who had previously doubted the Prophet on other decisions.

Sometime around 1831 Joseph had prayed to the Lord about the practice of ancient prophets marrying more than one woman. He had received the answer that this was part of the true covenant of marriage—an eternal form of marriage that eventually would be practiced in modern times. Joseph was apparently not eager to begin such a practice nor to teach it, but he did mention it privately to a few Church leaders. Somehow this knowledge spread, and the rumor began that polygamy was being taught and practiced in the Church. There actually may have been basis for the rumor, for Joseph was believed by some to have married Fanny Alger as a second wife in 1835.

Because of the rumors and other problems of the Saints in Kirtland, Joseph was much abused during the next few months. Numerous lawsuits were filed against him. Though he was always acquitted, the harassment became so threatening that at times he was even forced to leave the community. Emma dealt with the bill collectors and accusing apostates.

In the meantime, matters in Missouri also took a bad turn. Citizens in Clay County had felt sorry for the Saints when they had first been forced out of Jackson County. But now the Saints were increasing in numbers, buying land, and apparently planning to stay. A citizens' committee met in June 1836 and asked the Mormons to leave. Accusations against the Saints were the same as before: Mormons were easterners and nonslaveholders; they were poor; they were friendly to Indians; they had religious practices that were somewhat unusual to those who belonged to other churches.

But the people in Clay County were not so quick to use brutality as their neighbors in Jackson County. While some attacks did take place, the problem was settled simply by asking the Saints to leave. The old settlers reminded the Mormons that they had come as temporary guests.

The Saints had little choice. They did seek help in the state legislature through their friend and lawyer Alexander Doniphan. When the legislature offered to create a county in northern Missouri where few people lived and where the Saints would be left alone, this seemed the best answer. And so the Saints in Missouri were forced out of their homes once again. Some who had bought land were able to sell, but most sold at a great loss.

In Caldwell County, the town of Far West was established, and the Saints began to gather there. Once again, a whole city had to be built.

Joseph, during this time, was trying to keep the Church going in Kirtland, but the situation there was deteriorating.

Enemies brought various charges against him: that he had performed marriages without authority (Joseph knew he had authority from God, and he believed, as a minister, that he had authority from the state); that he had operated a bank without a charter (Joseph believed that his company had been legal as a joint stock operation); and that he owed money (this he did, but so did many persons in this time of economic crisis). Some of the most important leaders of the Church were also turning against the Prophet.

Early in 1838, Joseph received a revelation that his life was in danger, and that it was time for him to leave Kirtland. Soon the migration began. Loyal members of the Church—who still made up the majority—left Ohio throughout that year and headed west to northern Missouri. The Saints there had established a city, and now there would be a single gathering place.

GREATER TRIALS

The Saints hoped that the worst was now behind them. What they didn't know was that their trials had just begun. Living the gospel of Jesus Christ was challenge enough, but Mormons had no way of predicting that their way of life would create such bitter hatred among their neighbors.

This is not to say that the Saints were without fault. Early Mormons, including the Prophet Joseph, made their mistakes, as all humans do. But few people in American history ever paid so great a price merely to preserve their own existence.

CHAPTER 11

Far West

Joseph Smith and Sidney Rigdon fled from Kirtland together the night of January 12, 1838, traveled sixty miles to the town of Norton, and then waited for their families to catch up. Brigham Young had also fled. He and Joseph met in Dublin, Indiana.

Joseph was penniless. He considered seeking a job chopping wood to meet his needs on his journey to Missouri. But Brigham told him to wait; he was sure the Lord would provide. About that time a Brother Tomlinson in Dublin had the good fortune to get a good price for some property he had been trying to sell. When Brigham told him of the prophet's problems, Brother Tomlinson gave Brigham three hundred dollars, which Brigham passed on to Joseph. It was enough to get by for a couple of months.

The trip to Missouri included some frightening river crossings over ice that was breaking up, and some trying days in the extreme cold. One stretch of road was called "corduroy," a name settlers used for crude roads made of logs. Passing over the logs in a wagon could almost jar a rider's teeth loose. Five-year-old Joseph III later remembered some fun along the way—and some bad scares—but for Emma it was a dreadful ordeal. Julia might have helped some with Frederick, not yet two, but Emma was six months pregnant.

As the Prophet's group approached Far West, a brass band and a throng of Saints came out to greet them. Joseph loved such moments, but it was now especially satisfying to arrive in a place where everyone was so glad to have him.

Joseph was not sure he liked being a "settler." Life in Kirtland had been easier. But he built a log house, and he planted a garden. He also traveled about the area, meeting the Saints in other small settlements. It was at the Lyman Wight settlement, called Spring Hill, that he made a fascinating announcement. He discovered a curious pile of rocks, which he said was the remnant of a Nephite altar. (Nephites were ancient Americans described in the Book of Mormon.) But he also said that this was the area where Adam had blessed his posterity and where he would return to visit his people before the second coming of Christ. The rightful name of the place was Adam-ondi-Ahman.

In June, Emma gave birth to a boy—blond and blue-eyed, like Joseph. They named him Alexander Hale. Emma

Adam-ondi-Ahman

joked that she selected her own family name as a middle name because he was born in a "hale" storm.

Joseph's house was near the site set aside for a temple to be built. Nearby, Sidney Rigdon built a double-size log house that often served as a meetinghouse. Hyrum Smith, Joseph's beloved older brother, built a house just down the street. His wife, Jerusha, had died in Kirtland, and he had married an English woman named Mary Fielding, who accepted Hyrum's five children as her own.

Life seemed good again. Joseph loved it all: the green rolling hills of northern Missouri, the wooded ravines, the town laid out in neat blocks. He, as always, understood what the place could be. The town was nothing but log cabins—about 150 of them—with a few stores and mills, but he saw the temple that would stand where only a rough excavation was now visible. He saw the Saints spreading out over the hills in all directions, building communities according to God's plan—square towns, divided into blocks and lots, and surrounded by farms.

He had reason for optimism. What the Saints had accomplished in such a short time seemed proof of greater things to come. Most of those in Far West had come from the eastern states. Many of them were newly arrived on the frontier, where they had to adjust to the rigors of farming, to eating corn dodger and bacon, to living in one- or two-room cabins, and to accepting plank floors and window glass as luxuries. They were human, of course. They quarreled with their neighbors at times, lost patience with each other, sometimes even questioned decisions of their leaders. But they believed in a high purpose, and therefore they worked with commitment and accomplished more than anyone on these remote plains ever had before.

Sarah and Charles C. Rich married during this time and moved into a log house near Far West. Sarah's attitude was typical, as was her spelling: "We mooved to our coasey and happy home and we thought we ware the happyest couple in all the land. My husband had a beautifull prospect for a nice farm with plenty of timber and watter and our plans were laid for a comfortable and happy home in the near future our religion being first with us in all things."

The Saints in Missouri worked very hard, but they were happy. They loved the gospel and they loved the land they now possessed. They had little time for entertainment, but they were certainly not long-faced. They socialized when they could, and they looked forward to a time when they could again enjoy some of the cultural refinements they had left behind.

But the dreams and plans were not to be—at least not in Far West. Troubles were developing. Oliver Cowdery, David and John Whitmer, and William Phelps, who were all living in Far West, had begun to speak against the Church and the Prophet. They sold their Jackson County lands, against instruction. When the high council of Far West asked them to answer for this, they refused. They believed the council had no authority over them. After all, Oliver Cowdery was an assistant to President Joseph Smith, and the others had been set apart as the presidency in Missouri.

But the question ran deeper than the issue of line of authority. Did the Church—or the Prophet—have any right to instruct them in nonreligious matters? To Joseph, everything was spiritual. But to the dissenters, Joseph was overstepping his rights.

In June, Sidney Rigdon gave a sermon in which he compared the dissenters to salt that had lost its savor. The Bible said that such salt should be cast out and "trodden under the foot of men." As a result, a committee soon presented a petition to the dissenters asking that they leave town.

Until this time, many Missourians had seen the Mormons only as victims. But as word of the actions against the dissenters spread, the Saints were viewed for the first time in the role of aggressors. Many who had sided with the Mormons were drawn to the other side; those who had always hated the Mormons felt all the more justified.

About the same time, a secret military group was formed to protect the Saints in case of future enemy attacks. Joseph Smith knew about the organization, but he viewed it strictly as a defensive group. He did not know the extremes it would go to. Sampson Avard, the leader, preached the right of this little army, nicknamed Danites, to do virtually anything to protect the Church, even if it meant violence. During the few months the organization existed, it retaliated against non-Mormon forces, burning houses, stealing cattle—in fact, employing some of the same techniques used by the old settlers.

Few would doubt the right of the Saints to protect themselves, but the extreme doctrines of Sampson Avard, justifying almost any act in God's name, were dangerous to the Church. Eventually he would prove himself a coward, turning against the Saints to save himself, and he would be excommunicated. But for generations afterward the myth would persist that the Danites continued to exist.

The mood in northern Missouri was quickly changing. As more Saints arrived, old settlers were becoming openly resistant. All the old complaints were being spread again: the Mormons were fanatics; they would take over the region and elect their own officials; they would join forces with the Indians and attempt to drive the old settlers out. The Mormons must be stopped before their numbers grew any greater. And once again harassment began: insults, beatings, acts of vandalism.

But the Saints were also becoming confident of their

own strength. That summer their numbers swelled to 5,000. A militia was established and began to drill. The Saints would not be driven away so easily this time.

On July 4, 1838, the Church members put on a show of power. They marched their militia to the town square, parade style, and celebrated America's independence. Sidney Rigdon was the orator. He praised the nation in a rousing Fourth of July speech—in his usual flamboyant style—but then concluded with a vow. He said that the Saints had been trampled on, and they were weary of it. If a mob were to come against them again, he said, it would be "between us and them, a war of extermination; for we will follow them til the last drop of blood is spilled, or else they will have to exterminate us." And then he bellowed out his final proclamation: "Remember then, all men! We will never be the aggressors; we will infringe on the rights of no people, but shall stand for our own until death. . . . We this day proclaim ourselves free, with a purpose and a determination that never can be broken—No, never! No, never! NO NEVER!!!"

The audience cheered wildly, Joseph Smith among them, and the non-Mormons present seemed to accept the right of the Saints to resist aggression. But as the speech was printed in newspapers throughout the region, the harsh wording appeared to be a declaration of war. "A war of extermination," Sidney had said. Those words would come back to haunt the Saints.

More Mormons were arriving from Kirtland all the time. One large company of over five hundred, in a wagon train a mile long, started toward Far West in July. Their numbers were considerably reduced by the time they arrived, but they were all sent to settle in Adam-ondi-Ahman. The local residents there were not happy. Adam-ondi-Ahman was in Daviess County, and many old settlers believed that the

Saints had promised to settle only in Caldwell County. The Mormons argued that no American citizens could be denied the right to buy land and live in the place they chose, but the argument did not change the minds of those who were set against the Saints.

August 6, 1838, was election day in Missouri. William Peniston was running for the state legislature in Daviess County. He had hoped to befriend the Mormons and receive their votes, but the Mormons were well aware of his anti-Mormon activities of the past. Seeing that he could not gain support, then, he tried to stop all Mormons from voting. He excited a drunken group of men and persuaded them to interfere with the Mormons when they arrived at the polling place in Gallatin.

A Mormon was attacked by some of these ruffians, and soon a general melee was underway. At least one knife was used by an old settler, but no shots were fired. A Mormon named John Butler saved the day when he grabbed an oak-heart stick and began to "tap" the heads of the men in the mob. He said that he had no intention of killing anyone and that he wanted only to bring peace, but at the same time he was knocking down one after the other of the old settlers.

Both sides later claimed victory. Some of the Mormons did vote, but in the long run, they lost the battle. Exaggerated stories spread quickly that the Mormons were attacking. A false story also reached Joseph. Two brethren were reported to be dead, lying in the streets of Gallatin. He quickly gathered a group of men together and rode to Adam-ondi-Ahman, where he learned that the story was not true.

But Joseph was very concerned. He was not going to allow his people to be driven out of Daviess County by a bunch of rabble. He and Lyman Wight, with a sizable group of men, rode to the home of Adam Black, a judge, to lodge a complaint. The Mormons said that Judge Black tried to show his fairness by writing out an affidavit that he was un-attached to any mob, but he later claimed that he was forced at gunpoint to write the document.

William Peniston went to Judge Austin King in Rich-mond and swore a complaint that Mormons had threatened his life and vowed to take over the county by force. Judge King sent a sheriff to bring in Lyman Wight and Joseph Smith.

Accounts of all this, grossly overstated, reached the gov-ernor of Missouri. And the governor was none other than Lilburn Boggs, who had supported the mob throughout their actions in Jackson County. He dispatched General David Atchison, of the state militia in Liberty, to take a force into Caldwell and Daviess counties to attempt to quell the problems.

General Atchison recommended that Joseph Smith stand trial for the incident involving Justice Black. Joseph agreed to do so. The judge allowed him to go free on bail, and privately stated that there was no evidence against him, but this satisfied very few people in the state.

Missouri newspapers were filled with accounts of the "Mormon War." A few persons defended the Saints and ex-pressed fear that the incident would damage the state's repu-tation. Most, however, warned that the Mormons were out to conquer and rule all of Missouri.

Attacks on Mormon farms and small settlements con-tinued. The Saints were retreating into Far West and Adam-ondi-Ahman, the two largest communities. War seemed un-avoidable.

CHAPTER 12

The Extermination Order

With all that the early Latter-day Saints were forced to suffer, it would seem that life must have been grim and painful. But the journals written during those early years of the Church reveal not only a determined people, but also a people who enjoyed life and made the best of things, even in difficult times.

Joseph Smith often led the way in creating enjoyment for the people. Young Orange Wight, son of Lyman, wrote that when Joseph Smith and Sidney Rigdon visited his father in Adam-ondi-Ahman on one occasion, they all went swimming in the Grand River. He remembered much fun and laughter. Edward Stevenson recorded that on the very night that Joseph led his company of men to the Wight home, expecting to do battle after the incident at the elections in Gallatin, he got the men involved in a snowball fight for relaxation. Bathsheba Bigler, who was in her teens when the Saints made the difficult trip from Kirtland to Far West, and who later married George A. Smith, spoke of the "great fun" of crossing the prairies and hills and camping in tents at night. Luman Shurtliff wrote of his joy in hearing the cooing of prairie hens and the croaking of bullfrogs.

Even during the worst of times, young people got married, built homes, and began their families. Schools carried on. Boys swam and fished in the rivers. Young people went to the woods to find honey and gather nuts and berries. And when the Saints were driven from one place to another, their dolls and toys made the journey with them. The Saints believed in the future, and they made the best of hard times. Few times, however, were worse than those that came in the fall of 1838. Certainly, for a time, pleasure was in very short supply.

Early in the month of October, mobs surrounded and fired upon De Witt, a Mormon settlement on the Missouri River in Carroll County. The Saints there held out for a few days, but their supplies dwindled quickly. Joseph Smith rode to De Witt and sneaked into town to confer with them. He then wrote to Governor Boggs, pleading for help from state militia forces. Governor Boggs replied that the two sides would have to fight it out for themselves. Joseph had no choice but to negotiate. He did secure safe passage for his followers, but the promise of payment for lost homes and property was never kept.

Despite the snows and bitter cold, the Saints in De Witt had to leave their homes, angry with the injustice, but defeated and downcast. Most of them had eaten very little over the past few days. As they traveled north toward Far West, they rationed what few provisions were left. But all too many of them were sick and inadequately protected from the storm. Older people and children suffered the most; several died along the way. Zadoc Judd, just a boy, had no shoes but walked barefoot through the snow, herding three cows. Sister Downey, an older woman from Canada, died and was wrapped in a quilt and buried out on the plain.

Many of the De Witt Saints were taken into homes in Far West, but the town was filled to capacity with refugees from other areas. Charles and Sarah Rich, who had moved out of their little cabin into a house in town, took in seven extra families. Some people were reduced to sleeping in their wagons with nothing more than a blanket or two for protection. Sickness was everywhere. To make problems worse, food supplies were inadequate. As the Mormons in the countryside escaped to town, they abandoned crops or watched old settlers purposely destroy them. Many were forced to survive on boiled or hand-grated corn and pumpkins. Parents sacrificed so their children could eat, but the children still suffered from the cold and the lack of nutritious food.

Joseph, outraged by what was happening, called for volunteers to stand with him and resist the mob. He argued that the law would not protect the Saints, so they must protect themselves. Many volunteered, and these were added to the number already in the Far West militia.

Several Missouri militia units were now in the field, attempting to keep the peace. Some of these were led by men sympathetic to the Mormons; others were more mob than militia. For this reason, Joseph sent one hundred men to Adam-ondi-Ahman, to protect the Saints there.

Late one night Don Carlos Smith's wife, Agnes, trudged into Adam-ondi-Ahman, exhausted and half frozen. Her husband was on a mission in the southern states. A mob of men had come to her house and forced her out into the cold, allowing her to take nothing but her two little children. The mob had then stolen all her property and burned her house. She had walked three miles through the snow and waded the icy Grand River in waist-deep water.

Lyman Wight was furious. He went to General H. G. Parks, commander of one of the state militia units in the area, and demanded that such violence be stopped. General Parks told him to take his militia and disperse the mobs wherever he found them. But Lyman soon overstepped his authority. He marched into Gallatin with forty men, burned the store, and confiscated the goods.

During the next few days Lyman, as leader of the Danites in his settlement, was in open war with the old settlers in the neighborhood. He and his followers burned homes and confiscated cattle and other goods.

Word soon spread that the Mormons were attacking on all fronts and were beginning their war to conquer Missouri, and Governor Boggs authorized more troops. A man named Samuel Bogart, hearing rumors of attack, organized his own militia and began driving out Mormons who were still in their homes in southern Caldwell County. The militia was also reported to be holding three Mormons prisoner. When Mormon leaders learned of this, David W. Patten, the senior apostle, led a group of men to search for Bogart.

Elder Patten found Bogart's men camped on the Crooked River. Just at daybreak, the Mormons attacked, driving the Bogart militia away. Though one of Bogart's men was killed, the Mormon losses were much greater. Gideon Carter and Patrick O'Bennion were killed, and David W. Patten was mortally wounded.

In Far West a very sad funeral was held for Elder Patten, while in Jefferson City, Governor Boggs received reports describing the skirmish as a "Mormon massacre." He sent General John B. Clark into the field with this order: "The Mormons must be treated as enemies and must be exterminated or driven from the state." Sidney Ridgon's word, "extermination," was coming back to haunt the Saints.

Many Missouri settlers interpreted the extermination order as permission to murder. Three days after the order, a large group of men rode into a little settlement known as Haun's Mill. As the Mormons waved their hats and yelled that they wanted peace, the riders opened fire. Men,

The Haun's Mill Massacre

women, and children scattered into the woods or to the blacksmith shop, bullets flying all around them.

When it was all over, some sixteen hundred shots had been fired. Seventeen of the Mormons were dead, and thirteen more were wounded and left to suffer. Amanda Smith, who had been shot at, managed to hide in the woods. When she finally felt safe to come out, she found her husband and her ten-year-old son Sardius dead. Another son, seven-year-old Alma, had been shot in the hip and had saved himself only by pretending to be dead.

The dead were quickly buried in an old well, and those survivors who could travel left the settlement. Word of the massacre reached Joseph Smith in Far West, but by that time he was facing an army himself. Large numbers of troops had lined up south of Far West. Some were authorized militias; others were volunteer armies, itching for some action.

The Saints had torn down fences, even cabins, and

turned over wagons to create a barrier of defense. Behind it, they waited all night for the attack to come. Joseph encouraged them, telling them that there was no greater act of love than to give up one's life for friends—but gradually it became clear that his troops were hopelessly outnumbered. The Saints had every right to their land and to be protected—or to protect themselves—but a massacre was inevitable if they tried to fight.

Finally Joseph rode out with several other leaders, waving a white flag. He trusted that negotiations were to take place. Instead, he was taken captive. As the Mormons looked on, their leaders were taken back to the enemy camp, while the soldiers howled their approval. All night Joseph and the other Mormon captives—Sidney Rigdon, Lyman Wight, Parley Pratt, and George Robinson—were kept on the ground in a drenching rain. A court-martial was held, and the men were convicted of various crimes. In the morning, they were told that they would receive the death penalty. The group knelt together and prayed that their lives would be spared. In the meantime, Samuel Lucas, their captor, sent a message to General Alexander Doniphan informing him that he was to take the prisoners to the public square in Far West and shoot them.

General Doniphan was a friend of Joseph's. However, he was also an officer in the state militia, and he had received a direct order from a ranking officer. His courage was therefore remarkable. He returned a note to General Lucas, telling him, "It is cold-blooded murder. I will not obey your order. . . . If you execute these men, I will hold you responsible before an earthly tribunal, so help me God."

General Lucas backed down, and the men were not shot. But if their lives were saved for the moment, there was nothing else to be thankful for. The Mormon militia was forced to march out of town and lay down their weapons, and the

Saints were required to sign away all their possessions. In addition, the Mormons were all required to leave the state. They could stay through the winter, but come spring, should they attempt to stay, the extermination order would be carried out.

In spite of promises of protection, mobs rode through the town, harassing the people and destroying crops and homes. Emma Smith and her children were forced into the street while men ransacked the home and stole whatever they liked.

On November 2, Joseph Smith and the other prisoners were brought to Far West. They were allowed to go to their homes for their coats, but they were not given any time with their families. Little Joseph clung to his father's legs, sobbing, but a soldier thrust him away with the edge of his sword and told the boy that he would never see his father again.

Down the street, Hyrum Smith was pulled from a sickbed and taken away. His wife was about to have a baby. Parley Pratt's wife was sick and had a new baby to care for, but Parley too was taken away.

As the prisoners were taken to a wagon and confined, a crowd gathered around. Joseph's mother and his sister Lucy hurried to the area and were helped through the crowd. Joseph and Hyrum spoke to them and reached their hands out from under the wagon's cover. The two women held the hands, convinced that the two men would be put to death.

As the crowd watched in silence, the wagon rolled out of town. Rain was pouring down, and they stood in the mud, many of them crying. They assumed they had seen the last of Joseph and their other leaders.

As a final insult, General John Clark of the state militia assembled the Saints of Far West and addressed them. He denounced them for their behavior in the past and told them never to gather together again. "You are indebted to my clemency," he told them. "As for your leaders, do not think—do not imagine for a moment—do not let it enter your minds that they will be delivered, or that you will see their faces again, for their fate is fixed—their die is cast— their doom is sealed."

Fifty-six other Mormons were arrested—almost all the leadership in the Church—and General Clark must have been convinced that Mormonism was dead. Certainly almost everyone else in the state thought so too. And even the Saints themselves, quietly listening to General Clark's insults, must have wondered.

CHAPTER 13

Exodus to Illinois

Joseph Smith and the other Mormon leaders were taken to Independence and paraded before the citizens of Jackson County. Joseph wrote to Emma that he was treated well, which says more about Joseph than about the treatment. He and the other prisoners were locked in a vacant house for two nights and forced to sleep on the floor.

All the same, he was given considerable freedom, allowed to walk the streets at times and to converse freely with the townspeople. Both he and some non-Mormons reported his success at changing people's attitudes toward him. His friendly, open, and persuasive approach won him friends during the few days he was in Independence.

From Independence, the prisoners were taken to Richmond, Ray County, Missouri. Treatment there was much more harsh. The men were chained together and locked in a prison cell. Even though Sidney Rigdon was delirious with a fever, he was chained with the others and forced to sleep on the floor.

By now, many of the other Mormon leaders had also been brought to Richmond. Debate was raging over General Clark's authority to try the men. Unquestionably, he would have had the Mormons shot, but he finally accepted the argument that he had no jurisdiction over private citizens. The authority fell to Judge Austin King, who was to hold a civil court of hearing.

But Judge King was just as opposed to the Mormon leaders as was General Clark. He had even been at Far West on the night of the court-martial and had supported the death penalty. His procedures in court were clearly illegal. He allowed everyone who would speak against the Mormons to have their say. Several apostate Mormons used the opportunity to vent their frustrations or to save themselves.

When the Mormons, however, gave Judge King a list of forty men who could speak on their behalf, he promptly arrested the forty men and put them in jail. Very few were allowed to serve as witnesses, and those who did were harassed and not allowed to give full testimony. When the Saints turned over twenty more names for witnesses, all but one of the twenty could not be found. By now, they knew better than to go to Richmond, only to be jailed.

Finally Alexander Doniphan, who was again acting as legal counsel for the Saints, advised the Prophet to give up any attempt to deal with Judge King. It would be better to let the case go to trial than to prolong the unfair hearing.

But two weeks had passed, and the prisoners had suffered intensely in their cell, chained and forced to eat with their fingers. It was during this time that Parley Pratt observed one of Joseph's most powerful moments.

One night, as the prisoners tried in vain to sleep, the guards persisted in loudly relating disgusting stories of the treatment of the Mormons at Far West. They even joked about rapes, robberies, and murders.

Finally Joseph had heard enough. He rose to his feet, still in chains, and in a thundering voice denounced the guards in these words: "Silence! Ye fiends of the eternal pit! In the name of Jesus Christ I rebuke you, and command you to be still. I will not live another minute and hear such language. Cease such talk, or you or I die this instant!" Elder Pratt said that he had never before seen such majesty as he witnessed at that moment. The guards actually begged Joseph's pardon and were quiet the rest of the night.

On November 28, many of the Mormon leaders were released, but Joseph and Hyrum Smith, Sidney Rigdon, Lyman Wight, Alexander McRae, and Caleb Baldwin were sent to the town of Liberty, in Clay County, to be held for trial. Parley Pratt and several others were retained in Richmond.

Liberty Jail was a miserable prison. The prisoners were thrown into a damp basement heated only by smoky fireplaces. They slept on the floor on piles of straw. The ceiling was so low that Alexander McRae, who was six and a half feet tall, could not stand up straight. Even worse, they were forced to eat disgusting and filthy food. Often the prison guards joked about feeding them human flesh, and once the men were convinced they had been poisoned.

In such conditions, it would not have been surprising had Joseph and his companions become bitter and angry, but, in fact, the humbling experience seemed to bring out some of the best in them. Joseph had time to think and pray and to receive important revelations. His compassion deepened; his wisdom grew.

Joseph turned thirty-three that winter. Much had happened in only nine years since the Church had been organized. He had expected wonders; perhaps he had foreseen trials. But it was the anguish and pain of so many innocent converts to the faith that most deeply troubled him. When he called on God and asked how much longer the agony must continue, he received this answer: "My son, peace be unto thy soul; thine adversity and thine afflictions shall be but a small moment; and then, if thou endure it well, God shall exalt thee on high; thou shalt triumph over all thy foes."

What followed this promise was one of the most profound revelations Joseph was to receive. The Saints, he was told, would not be destroyed. But they must live in righteousness to receive all the blessings the Lord had in store for them. Priesthood authority must be administered "by gentleness and meekness, and by love unfeigned." The Spirit, he was taught, withdraws from those who live unrighteously, and therefore, "many are called, but few are chosen."

Joseph wrote many letters to Emma during this time. He sent his love to young Joseph, Julia, Frederick, and Alexander. He told them to be good children and to think of him. He promised that he would return.

Emma was able to visit Joseph three times that winter, accompanied by the wives of the other prisoners. These were some of the happiest times for the men. They stayed up all night, talked and sang, and "feasted on the spirit." Once young Joseph came with Emma, and the Prophet gave him a father's blessing. After one of the visits, Emma returned to Far West and found that her house had been broken into by a group of men led by William McLellin, one-time apostle, now apostate. They had taken almost everything of value.

Joseph continued to direct the affairs of the Church as best he could. He met with Church leaders, and he sent instructions. But most of the work of moving the Saints from Missouri was directed by Brigham Young and Heber C. Kimball. Because these two apostles had been away on missions during much of the time the Saints were in Far West, they were not as well-known and had not been jailed with the others.

Almost all the wealth of the Saints was in the land and

The Saints leaving Missouri

homes they possessed. But these they were forced to leave behind, rarely receiving compensation for them. Food was scarce, for their crops had been pillaged or destroyed by mobs. Brigham Young directed the distribution of the meager provisions, so everyone had a share. The Saints built wagons and organized small companies, but most of them traveled individually, making their way across the state as best they could. Many left in the winter, aware that the roads would turn into mud when spring came.

But the cold and the lack of adequate food took their toll. Many of the Saints, particularly children, died and had to be buried in crudely marked graves across Missouri.

Sarah Rich, pregnant and sick, fled with her friend Surmantha Stout, who was also very ill. Accompanying them were Sarah's father and a few other Saints. Sarah spent most of the journey in the back of a wagon, suffering almost unbearable pain as it bumped and jostled over the frozen ground. At the Mississippi River, the ice was beginning to flow, making a crossing treacherous. With Sarah expecting to deliver her baby at any time and no way even to get inside for warmth, their situation was desperate.

Sarah's and Surmantha's husbands, Charles C. Rich and Hosea Stout, had been forced to flee Far West earlier and were waiting for them on the Illinois side of the river. They decided to risk the crossing, and managed to bring the stranded party to safety in Illinois. Sarah described the experience: "Just think of it my dear reader to see us undertake such a perilous trip across the watter running with ice the cakes of which ware so large that some times the men would have to jump out on the ice in order to puch [push] it away and then jump back into the canoe again. . . . And my poor old father . . . stood with tears in his eyes watching us, not knowing whether we could rech [reach] shore or not."

Sarah was taken into a home in Illinois and gave birth to her baby soon after. Her health returned. Surmantha Stout was not so fortunate; she died a short time later.

When the Saints were forced out of their homes in Missouri, they were not sure where they were going. To the west was Indian country. To the north were the wilds of the mostly unsettled territory of Iowa. That was unsatisfactory, for if they were going to press legal action against Missouri, they would have to live in a state. Therefore, most of them headed east, across the Mississippi. By far the largest number found refuge in the area of Quincy, Illinois.

The people of Illinois took in literally thousands of the Latter-day Saints and gave them temporary quarters, jobs, and food. The state of Illinois needed settlers to strengthen its economy, so government leaders were only too happy to see new people move in. But even more, the people in Illinois saw the condition of the Saints and took pity on them.

All through the late winter and spring, the Mormons made their way to the Mississippi and crossed over. When Emma Smith reached the river in February, she was afraid the ice was not thick enough to cross safely. She walked apart from the wagon, carrying two-year-old Frederick and baby Alexander in her arms. She was also carrying Joseph's important papers, strapped around her waist. Julia clung to her skirt on one side, Joseph on the other. It was a long and frightening walk across the vast plain of ice, but they arrived safely in Illinois. A family named Cleveland took them into their home near Quincy.

In February Sidney Rigdon was released from the Liberty Jail, probably because of his frailty and illness. This was the first sign that Governor Boggs was embarrassed by the negative news stories about his state's treatment of the Mormons. This probably explains what happened on April 15. Joseph and the remaining prisoners had been taken to Gallatin, Daviess County, to stand trial. There they were told they were to be moved again, to Boone County. Soon after leaving Gallatin, the sheriff told Joseph that he was going to take a strong drink and go to bed. Joseph could do as he pleased. One of the guards helped the prisoners saddle two horses, and the five men escaped that night, three of them on foot. They headed immediately for safety in Illinois.

Parley Pratt and the other prisoners also escaped, and so no Mormon was ever put to death by the state of Missouri. Over the next few years, the Saints tried many times to receive compensation for their losses. They petitioned the United States Congress, the President, and the courts, and many expressed sympathy for their cause. But at that time, the federal government had a policy of staying out of almost all state-level disputes, and the issue was simply returned to Missouri officials for settlement. The Missouri legislature authorized a little money to help the Saints leave, but beyond this, the Saints lost everything they had owned there. Nonetheless, most of the Saints remained committed and loyal to the Church.

Drusilla Hendricks had seen her husband shot at Crooked River, handicapped for life; had lost her home in Clay County; and now had lost everything she owned in Caldwell County. She and her children lived in terror as they were repeatedly harassed by mobs and then forced to flee despite her husband's illness. Yet after all this, Drusilla was able to write: "We were in a strange land among strangers. The conflict began in my mind: 'Your folks told you your husband would be killed, and are you not sorry you did not listen to them?' I said, No I am not. I did what was right. If I die I am glad I was baptized for the remission of my sins, for I have an answer of a good conscience. But after that a third person spoke. It was a still small voice this time saying, 'Hold on, for the Lord will provide.' I said I would, for I would trust and not grumble."

By April 20, 1839, almost all of the Mormons had left Far West. Those who remained were mostly old or sick people who had not yet been able to move. But another attack on Far West forced even those people to leave. More property was destroyed, and the old and feeble were abused, but the old settlers had their final victory.

Or so they thought. Six days later several members of the Quorum of the Twelve Apostles rode into Far West at night. The previous summer Joseph Smith had received a revelation that on April 26, 1839, the apostles would leave on a mission to Europe from the site of the temple. Enemies of the Church had claimed that this was one revelation that would not be fulfilled.

At the site that had been selected for the temple, the brethren held a meeting. Wilford Woodruff and George A. Smith were ordained as apostles, to fill two vacant positions in the Twelve. The men rolled a stone into a corner place, to symbolize the laying of the foundation of the temple, and then each in turn prayed. To some it seemed a pointless gesture, but to Brigham Young and the other members of the Twelve, it was a way of saying that the work would go on, that the Church could not be destroyed by the forces of evil.

The men knew that they were in peril of their lives, but it was that very act of defiance that gave them the strength to face the difficult challenges ahead. Their mission to Europe would take place. The Saints were scattered and destitute, but they were not about to give up their dream of Zion.

When the apostles arrived in Illinois, they were reunited with Joseph Smith at the Cleveland home near Quincy. It was a joyous reunion. The Prophet had always said that he would be delivered from the jail—the Lord had promised it. Now it seemed possible to rebuild and continue the work of the Church. At the time they did not know exactly where, but they would begin to gather again, and they would re-establish Zion.

CHAPTER 14

Establishing Nauvoo

While the Saints were looking for a place to locate, a man by the name of Isaac Galland contacted Joseph Smith and said that he believed in the Mormon cause. He claimed to own a great deal of land in Iowa, as well as a sizable farm near Commerce, Illinois. He was willing to grant the Saints credit and make the land available immediately.

Joseph, with the approval of other Church leaders, decided to take the offer. They would build a new gathering place, with settlements on both sides of the Missouri River. The Church purchased the Galland farm near Commerce, as well as a farm from Hugh White. The name of the town the Mormons established there became "Nauvoo," a word that Joseph said came from the Hebrew, meaning "city beautiful."

The Prophet and his family moved into a small log home near the river. What he saw around him was the great arch of a bend in the mighty river, a beautiful site for a city. The land was thick with trees and underbrush, and high bluffs provided magnificent views out over the river. Though much of the area was swampy, Joseph believed that the Saints could drain the swamps and clear the land. As always, he saw what could be, not just what was. He envisioned an orderly city with a temple on the bluffs, spacious building lots with garden plots, and farms around the perimeter.

What he didn't realize was that the swamps bred mosquitoes, and though scientists had not yet discovered it, mosquitoes were a source of malaria. In the summer of 1839, many of the Mormons fell ill. By July the epidemic had spread to both sides of the river.

Joseph Smith himself fell ill, as did several others in his home. Despite his fever and sickness, Joseph pulled himself from his sickbed and blessed his own family members, commanding them to arise and walk. Then he went from home to home, tent to tent, along both sides of the river, blessing and comforting those who were afflicted. On the Iowa side, he blessed Brigham Young and other apostles who had established homes there. Elijah Fordham was critically ill, and his family thought he was in the last stages of the sickness. After

Malaria epidemic at Nauvoo

the Prophet commanded, in the name of Jesus Christ, that he arise, Elijah stood up immediately, made whole.

As Joseph was about to cross the river to return to Nauvoo, a man rushed up to him and reported that his twin daughters were dying. The Prophet took a handkerchief from his pocket and gave it to Wilford Woodruff, a member of the Twelve, telling him to go to the twins and to wipe their foreheads with it. He promised that they would be healed. Elder Woodruff did as he was told, and the twins recovered immediately.

Not everyone could be healed, however. Many died, if not the first summer, the second or third. Joseph suffered the grief of seeing some of the people closest to him die of the disease: his father, his younger brother Don Carlos, and his close friend and secretary Robert Thompson. Eventually, as the swamps were drained, the health of the community was greatly improved.

In the midst of all the challenges—a city to build, hundreds of refugees to house before winter, swamps to drain, land to clear—the apostles prepared to depart for their mission to England. John Taylor and Wilford Woodruff left in August 1839, both so sick they could hardly stand. Later that month apostles Parley Pratt and Orson Pratt, accompanied by Hiram Clark, departed.

Brigham Young and Heber C. Kimball followed them in September. The families of both were down with illness, and Brigham's wife had recently given birth. The apostles themselves were no better off. Each had only one worn-out suit of clothes, and Brigham was wrapped in a quilt because he had no overcoat. And both were very sick. Brigham could not walk without help. "My firm resolve," he later wrote, "was that I would do what I was required to do in the gospel of life and salvation, or I would die trying to do it."

Survival was not easy for the families of the missionaries.

George A. Smith's wife, Bathsheba, struggled with being alone, with only her baby to keep her company. She wrote many letters to her husband in the eastern states, where he was serving. She reported on conditions at home—the garden, the well, the health of their cow—and the growth of their son, George Albert. She described conditions in Nauvoo, naming the many people who were sick and those who had died.

Bathsheba Smith was managing, and she was committed to the importance of her husband's mission, but she also missed him terribly, as this letter shows: "O how I wish you could take dinner and chat an hour or two with us at least. We have been to the post office again and again but cannot get one word from you. How I do wish I did know you were well. I think I will get a letter tomorrow. I expected one certain last Wednesday. . . . I thought you must be sick or you would have written, for I have been uneasy about you for you had to ride in the rain so much."

Despite the great sacrifices of the missionaries and their families, the time was right for their missions. The Lord truly blessed their efforts. During the first ten years of the British mission, 17,849 converts were baptized. The British people, especially the laboring classes in the industrial cities, were ready for the message of these powerful men.

Many of the new converts made plans almost immediately to immigrate to America to join the main body of the Saints. Others started saving their money so they could emigrate later. Those who arrived in Nauvoo in the early 1840s may have been disappointed to find only the skeleton of a city in a muddy bottomland. But they knew that the Church was true and that the Lord would bless them, so they pitched in to help make the dream of a beautiful gathering place for the Saints come true.

Eventually Nauvoo became one of the largest cities in

what was then the frontier of the West. The towns on the west side of the river, in Iowa, however, did not prosper in the same way. As it turned out, Isaac Galland did not own clear title to the land he had sold the Saints. Many who moved there lost the money they had paid, as well as the investment in improvements.

But if Galland hurt the Church, his injuries were small compared to those of a man named John C. Bennett. And yet Bennett, like Galland, first came to the Saints as a friend. As an Illinois politician and man of some education, he impressed Joseph Smith, and he made many promises. At first, his promises were kept. He was instrumental in getting the state legislature to approve a carefully designed city charter for Nauvoo.

The style of government in Nauvoo—with most of the control in the hands of a few Church leaders—and the provision for a large militia would eventually become a sore point with the Illinois public. For the present, however, John C. Bennett seemed to be a friend that the Church needed. He came to Nauvoo, accepted baptism in the Church, and before long was voted mayor of the city.

For a time, Nauvoo did very well. In spite of the illness and the economic depression in the country, the economy of the city improved steadily. Illinois neighbors were friendly and uncritical of the Mormon way of life. The Church was able to borrow funds in order to erect buildings, and with such tremendous growth, there was work for everyone. A remarkable spirit of cooperation grew between the people who came from many diverse backgrounds: New Englanders, southerners, English, Welsh, Scots, Scandinavians, even some freed slaves.

Life in Nauvoo gradually became very pleasant, with Joseph and Emma Smith at the center of the social life. Their large new home served also as an inn or hotel. Joseph always made visitors feel welcome. He enjoyed explaining the principles of the gospel to newspaper writers, potential converts, or the merely curious. Riverboats often put in at Nauvoo, which became a significant landmark along the Mississippi. Nauvoo was known for its order and beauty.

Children in the city had plenty of chores to do, and school attendance kept them occupied much of the year. But there was also time to play. They enjoyed throwing quoits, a game much like horseshoes; they fished and swam in the river and explored the woods. And there was the wharf to visit, where the world passed by—immigrants, preachers, tourists, riverboat roustabouts, gamblers, Indians, foreigners.

The city was divided into sections, or wards, for voting. The term *ward* was gradually used to describe congregations of the Church. At first, church meetings were held in homes or, when the weather was nice, outdoors. The Prophet often preached to huge gatherings. He loved to explain Church doctrines, sometimes in lengthy sermons, and his understanding of the plan of salvation was enlarging as the Lord guided and instructed him. He preached that every person existed with God before this life, and that the purpose of all existence is eternal progress. This never-ending process of growth could lead to a person's reaching perfection in a future life and the possibility of becoming a god to some other world. These doctrines gave the Saints a sense of purpose and destiny.

Joseph was busy with all the activities of the community, both church and civic. In the fall of 1839, he traveled to Washington, D.C., to try to persuade the President and Congress to force the state of Missouri to pay for the Saints' losses there. In response to his pleas, he received sympathy but no help. He returned to Nauvoo to build a kingdom of God there that in many ways would be separate from the government of the nation.

By 1841, a university, primarily for adult education, was

established in Nauvoo. The university had no campus, but classes were held. There were also, in time, other cultural groups, such as debate and literary clubs, libraries, choirs, and bands.

On March 17, 1842, the Female Relief Society was formed, with Emma Smith as president. The members were organized to help provide for the needy, but Joseph also advised them to "provoke the brethren to good works." Many of the women reported in their diaries that through the sisters, miracles were performed, such as healings and the gift of tongues, and sisterhood in the Church greatly increased.

In the following year the Young Gentlemen and Ladies Relief Society of Nauvoo was also formed for young adults. Heber C. Kimball often spoke to the members. He advised them to think of more than parties and entertainments, to be aware of the needs of the people.

That did not mean that the young people should not enjoy themselves. Joseph Smith loved wholesome entertainments, and now that his days were not spent in combating enemies, he could find time for such pleasures. He enjoyed athletic contests, and many of the Saints recorded that they witnessed him wrestling, running races, jumping, pulling sticks, and romping with the children.

Some persons who came to Nauvoo were amazed to find such a down-to-earth, almost playful person as the leader of the Church. Wilford Woodruff said of his first meeting with Joseph, "It might have shocked the faith of some men. I found him and his brother Hyrum out shooting at a mark with a brace of pistols." Joseph wrote in his journal about "taking a little air" while horseback riding, or sliding on the ice with "my little Frederick." He sometimes held a wood-cutting "bee" when his supply of firewood was low. He and the men he invited would compete in sawing, chopping, splitting, and stacking the wood.

Joseph Smith addressing the Nauvoo Legion

Joseph loved to be with people. He liked weddings and parties and dances and dinners. He enjoyed the time he spent with Emma and their children, and he often walked the streets to talk to people. Perhaps as much as anything, he enjoyed riding his white stallion at the head of a parade. As the lieutenant general of the Nauvoo Legion, he held the highest military rank in the United States—at least in name—and he would put on a fancy blue-and-white uniform, trimmed with gold braid, strap on his sword, and mount his beautiful horse.

But if Joseph loved life, that did not detract from his serious spiritual mission. During this period, the Lord revealed to him the full purpose of temples, special buildings where only worthy members of the Church could go to perform sacred ordinances. Adult members of the Church could participate in a special endowment ceremony; they would make promises to God that they would fully commit themselves to his kingdom, and in return, they would be given eternal blessings. Marriages could be sealed in the temples for eternity, and children could also be sealed to their parents for eternity. But the blessings were not just for the living. Persons who had died could have these earthly ordinances performed in their behalf, and family members could be sealed from generation to generation in an eternal chain.

Early in 1841, Joseph received a revelation that a temple should be built in Nauvoo. He had already seen the place for it, on the bluffs overlooking the city. The temple would be the symbol of the city: not just another town along the river, but a city of holiness, a gathering place for those committed to serving God.

CHAPTER 15

The Martyrdom

In the first years of Nauvoo's settlement, local citizens spoke highly of their new Mormon neighbors. But once again, attitudes began to change. And the complaints were very much like the ones Mormons had heard before.

Mormons soon outnumbered the non-Mormon citizens of Hancock County, Illinois. This gave them political and economic power, for they could assure that Mormons would be elected to important county positions. The small towns in the county suddenly lost power, as Nauvoo quickly became one of the biggest cities in the state. The older citizens also saw a pattern of mixing church and state in a way that seemed somehow un-American. Most civic positions in Nauvoo were held by leading Church authorities. As far as non-Mormons were concerned, the Prophet had entirely too much power.

There were also problems in state politics. When the Mormons first arrived in Illinois, politicians hurried to seek favor and to win the new voters over to their own party's side. While this helped win favors for the Mormons at first, politicians who failed to win such crucial support soon became angry. As the Mormon population grew, both sides began to fear the power of such a large, unified bloc of voters.

A man named Thomas Sharp was the first opponent to express such views publicly. The editor of the small-town newspaper, the *Warsaw Signal,* he began as early as 1841 to warn readers of the dangers of Mormon power. Other newspapers picked up the cry. When Mr. Sharp ran against William Smith, the Prophet's brother, for the state legislature, he lost the election—which only increased his hatred for the Mormons. Eventually he began calling for Joseph's death and the extermination of the Saints. These were familiar words to the Saints, who had survived the ordeal in Missouri, but they were not words they had expected from Illinois.

Other events heated up the hateful feelings. John C. Bennett had become one of the most important figures in Nauvoo, the mayor and a close associate of Joseph Smith. But in 1842 the Prophet discovered that Bennett had been attempting to use the doctrine of plural marriage to persuade young women to enter into immoral relationships. He also found that Bennett had lied about his past. He was married and had abandoned his family in the East. As a result, he was excommunicated from the Church and removed as mayor of Nauvoo, but he became one of the bitterest enemies of the Church.

John C. Bennett set about to damage the Church in every way he could. He wrote a book against the Saints, a book that combined truths with half-truths and lies. He was soon speaking throughout the state, doing what he could to stir public sentiment against the Church.

One of Bennett's accusations was that the Mormons were practicing polygamy. Joseph Smith had earlier learned through revelation from God that ancient prophets had been married to more than one woman and that this principle, to be known as eternal or celestial marriage, would return with the restoration of other ancient doctrines. He taught the doctrine to the apostles when they returned from England.

"The principle," as plural marriage came to be known, was not easy for the apostles to accept. One after another, however, they became converted to the principle as part of the "restoration of all things," and they accepted their responsibility to live it. John C. Bennett, of course, saw nothing eternal or spiritual in the principle, and the rumors he spread heightened the feelings against the Mormons.

In 1842, an unknown assailant shot former governor Boggs of Missouri in the back of the head. When he recovered, he accused Orrin Porter Rockwell, Joseph's cousin and bodyguard, of the shooting, and Joseph of instigating the crime. Missouri authorities tried to arrest Joseph, but he was released by the municipal court in Nauvoo, whose judges were Latter-day Saints. Their intent was to protect him from being returned to Missouri, where he was likely to be killed, but the judges extended their powers beyond usual court procedures.

Understandably, the non-Mormon citizens of Illinois accused the Mormon-controlled courts in Nauvoo of abusing their power. No Mormon could be convicted of anything if his brethren had license to protect him, they claimed. The evidence seemed clear that there was real danger in mixing church and state.

Joseph, who recognized these problems, began to consider various options for the Saints. Perhaps they should leave the United States entirely and head into a western territory where they could establish their own society and run it as they chose. He also saw good reason for establishing a government guided by men of God. As a result, he established a Council of Fifty, a group under priesthood leadership, to become a governing body in the community.

Joseph believed that the political parties of the United

States had strayed far from true principles. He therefore decided in early 1844 to create a new party and to run for U.S. President as a candidate of that party. To organize the party, he called missionaries to go forth to both preach the gospel and campaign for his candidacy. He developed a platform on which to campaign, presenting practical solutions to current problems. The basis of his platform was the proposal that a man of God should lead the nation. All of America was Zion, he taught, and the country needed spiritual direction.

But neither the campaign nor the plans to move west would progress much further in the Prophet's own lifetime.

Several men in Nauvoo, including some important leaders, disagreed with Joseph over some of the Church's teachings, including plural marriage. They left the Church but stayed in the community, and in early June they began to publish an anti-Mormon newspaper, the *Nauvoo Expositor*. They denounced Joseph Smith as a fallen prophet and accused him of all sorts of crimes and character flaws.

Loyal Mormons were shocked by these accusations. They were also fearful of the division and hatred that would be created by the newspaper. The city council met and, in the name of a "public nuisance" law, proclaimed the newspaper illegal. Joseph Smith, as mayor, then ordered the paper destroyed. When news of this action reached surrounding towns, the people were outraged. The Mormons argued that they had been subjected to enough lies. They were not going to allow the newspaper to continue to publish such falsehoods. But this argument was not heard.

The publishers of the newspaper obtained an arrest warrant against the Prophet, but once again the court released him. Joseph could see that trouble was ahead. He placed the city under martial law and assembled the Nauvoo Legion. This time, he vowed, his army would fight if necessary. He also wrote to Governor Thomas Ford and asked for an investigation.

Rumors quickly spread that Joseph Smith had proclaimed war on the communities around Nauvoo. Preparations for war began on both sides. In Nauvoo, the Saints dug trenches and placed guards on all roads. The non-Mormons formed a posse to defend themselves.

Governor Ford seemed willing at first to hear the Church's side of the argument. He traveled to Carthage, the county seat, to find out what was going on. It soon became evident to the Prophet, however, that the Governor was not really listening. When non-Mormon forces persisted in trying to arrest Joseph, he finally decided to leave Nauvoo and cross the river into Iowa. He reasoned that his enemies wanted him and his brother Hyrum, and that if they left, the Saints in Nauvoo would be safe.

Joseph and Hyrum, with the help of Porter Rockwell and Willard Richards, crossed the river in the early hours of Sunday, June 23, 1844. Later that day, they received reports that the Saints were in a state of confusion and worried about what to do should fighting break out. Even worse, some of his followers were complaining that Joseph had run to save himself.

This was too much for Joseph. He told Porter, "If my life is of no value to my friends, it is of none to myself." He wrote to Governor Ford and told him that he would give himself up. Then he and Hyrum crossed the river back to Illinois.

On Monday, June 24, Joseph and seventeen other men who had been charged with crimes left Nauvoo for Carthage, where warrants had been issued for their arrest. A company of the Saints rode with them to provide protection. As the group was leaving town, Joseph stopped and looked back at the city and the temple. "This is the loveliest place and the best people under the heavens," he said. "Little do they know the trials that await them."

On the way to Carthage, the riders were met by a state militia. Governor Ford had ordered that the Nauvoo Legion give up its state weapons. Joseph, to show his good faith, sent one of his men back to carry out this order. He then returned, with the Illinois militia, to make certain the order was carried out.

As he turned back toward Carthage that evening, Joseph seemed to know what lay ahead. He told his followers, "I am going like a lamb to the slaughter, but I am calm as a summer's morning. I have a conscience void of offense toward God and toward all men."

On Tuesday morning, the Mormons were arrested in Carthage. After posting bail, they were released. But late that evening, Joseph and Hyrum Smith were again arrested, this time on a charge of treason. They decided to go to jail; with hundreds of angry anti-Mormon militiamen now in Carthage, they would probably be safer there than in a hotel.

Governor Ford, to his credit, seemed to be seeking a resolution to the problem without bloodshed. When he heard that anti-Mormon forces were heading for Nauvoo, he went there himself to try to head off further difficulties. He found things calm in Nauvoo, despite rumors that the Saints were preparing to attack. But he had left Joseph and Hyrum virtually defenseless at Carthage.

On Thursday, June 27, Joseph and Hyrum, who were still in jail, had breakfast with three friends who chose to be with them—Willard Richards, John Taylor, and Stephen Markham. Joseph wrote a letter to Emma, telling her that he had "done the best that could be done," and expressing love for his family and all his friends. He and Hyrum bore testimony to their companions, reaffirming their belief in the divinity of the work of the Church.

After lunch, Willard Richards felt ill, so Stephen Markham was sent out for some medicine. As soon as he left the jail, angry guards threw him on a horse and drove him out of town.

The Carthage Jail

As the hot summer afternoon wore on, the guards became more abusive and began to argue among themselves. Outside an angry mob was gathering. The prisoners, in an upstairs cell, looked out and saw men with mud daubed on their faces. Shortly after five o'clock, two or three gunshots rang out and the prison guards were overpowered by the mob. Angry men with guns charged up the stairs to the room where Joseph and his companions were trapped. Bullets also began to fly through the windows from outside.

Hyrum was struck first, in the face. As he fell, he exclaimed, "I am a dead man!" Then two other bullets hit him in the back. Joseph, stunned, cried, "Oh, my dear brother Hyrum!"

Joseph had a six-shooter that had been smuggled into the jail. He fired the gun toward the stairs, while Willard Richards used his cane and John Taylor used a hickory stick to knock down rifles thrust through the partially open door. The mobbers retreated for a moment, then came back up the stairs and opened fire again. Suddenly John Taylor fell and rolled under the bed. He had been struck by five bullets.

The Prophet ran to the window, seeking some means of escape, but bullets continued to fly at him from both inside and outside. He jumped to the window, paused for a moment, and cried, "Oh Lord, my God!" Then he fell to the ground below, dead. When they realized the Prophet had fallen through the window, the attackers in the jail ran outside.

Back in the jail cell, Willard Richards escaped with only a minor nick in the ear. John Taylor, though badly hurt, would recover from the vicious attack. Later that evening Elder Richards sent word back to Nauvoo, informing the Saints that the Prophet and his brother were dead.

In Nauvoo, the Saints went into deep mourning for their beloved leader. Across the state of Illinois, non-Mormon citizens prepared for an attack by the Mormons, fearing they would seek revenge. But the Saints mourned their loss quietly and with dignity.

Once the enemies of the Church discovered that the Saints were not going to fight, they became convinced that the Mormon movement would dissolve. Without Joseph Smith, they assumed, there was no prophet to follow, no way to carry on. That, however, was not to be the case. Joseph had sealed his testimony with his blood. He had given the ultimate testimony that what he had seen and heard—angels, even God himself—was indeed true. That testimony would be a great strength and reassurance for the Latter-day Saints for generations to come.

THE KINGDOM IN THE WEST

What the Saints needed, if they were to survive, was a strong leader. The Lord had prepared just the man. Brigham Young was as tough as he was tender. He had the right combination of talents to lead a people to a desert and to turn it into a garden.

The Saints would never give up on the idea that Jackson County, Missouri, was still Zion. They knew it would still play a role in the future of the Church. But for now the Saints would be forced to take what they could get, and that was a barren desert that no one else wanted. The hardships were not over; they had only just begun. But peace seemed a possibility, and the Saints were willing to suffer much to get to a place where they might be left alone.

CHAPTER 16

The Loss of Nauvoo

On June 28, 1844, the bodies of Joseph and Hyrum Smith were carried back to Nauvoo, each in a rough pine box. The Nauvoo brass band met the wagon and, along with an honor guard of twelve men, led the procession into the city. Thousands lined the streets, most shedding tears, as the wagon slowly made its way to Joseph's home, the Mansion House.

The families of the two martyrs were overcome with grief. Emma fainted when she first tried to draw near to Joseph's body. Finally she was able to look at Joseph. "Oh, Joseph, Joseph," she sobbed. "My husband, my husband! Have they taken you from me at last?" Mary Fielding, Hyrum's wife, put her head upon her husband's chest and cried, with her sorrowing children gathered around her.

Lucy Mack Smith, the Prophet's mother, arrived. "My God, my God," she wept, "why hast thou forsaken this family!" She stood between her sons, resting a hand on each, and shook with grief.

The next day the bodies were viewed by ten thousand Latter-day Saints. All day they filed through the living room, where the bodies lay. Men, women, and children

sobbed as they said their final farewell to the leaders they
had loved so much. Joseph had been their prophet, their
preacher, their spiritual strength, but he had also been a
brother and friend. His exhilarating power and optimism
had carried them through many trials. And Hyrum, the
steady, loyal brother, had always stood beside Joseph in
carrying out the work of the Church.

One woman, Sally Randall, wrote to her non-Mormon
relatives: "If you can imagine to yourselves how the apostles
and saints felt when the Savior was crucified you can give
something of a guess how the Saints felt here when they
heard that their prophet and patriarch were both dead and
murdered, too, by a lawless mob. . . . The earth is deprived
of the two best men on it. They have sealed their testimony
with their blood."

Most of the apostles were serving missions, preaching
the gospel and campaigning for Joseph's candidacy for President. Brigham Young was in Boston on what had been for
him a difficult mission. While he was away, he had received
word that his six-year-old daughter, Mary Ann, had died.
During her father's many missions, she had always refused to
go to bed until she had prayed for him. Brigham had loved
her dearly.

He was already grieved by this loss, not feeling well, and
missing his family when rumors reached him that the
Prophet had been murdered. It was July 16 before he received confirmation that the rumors were true. His first
thought, he said, was whether or not Joseph had taken the
keys of authority with him. But he remembered what had
happened a few months before, on March 26, 1844.

On that day Joseph had met with some of the Church
leaders to further organize the Council of Fifty. He had told
the brethren that some important event was about to take
place, that perhaps he would be killed, and that he must pass

the keys of authority on to the apostles. He committed those keys to the Twelve on that day. Remembering this, Brigham Young felt reassured. The loss of the Prophet was cause for sorrow, but the Church would go on.

As soon as word of the martyrdom reached the apostles, they began their journeys back to Nauvoo. Brigham Young and several others arrived in Nauvoo on August 6. Two days before, on August 4, Sidney Rigdon had spoken to the Saints at an outdoor assembly and had made his case that he should lead the Church. Actually, he had hastened back to Nauvoo from Pittsburgh. Before the murder, he had left Nauvoo, disillusioned with Joseph's leadership. Joseph had wanted to release him from the First Presidency some months before; however, Sidney had pleaded to be retained in office, and the members of the Church had voted for his continued service.

Until now, the Saints had thought very little about the passing of the mantle of authority. A special conference was called for August 8 to consider the matter. Fortunately, Brigham Young and the other apostles arrived in time.

At the meeting, Sidney Rigdon spoke first. It was a blustery day, with the wind blowing from behind the congregation, and so he had gone to the back and stood on a wagon. All had turned on their benches to hear him. He argued that Joseph Smith would always be the Prophet. But now a "guardian" was needed, he said, and he claimed that he, Sidney Rigdon, had been called by God to speak for the Prophet.

Just before President Rigdon began to speak, Brigham Young had arrived and sat down on the stand in front with other Church leaders. Few people saw him; in fact, many did not know that he was back in Nauvoo. At the conclusion of Sidney's remarks, Brigham arose and spoke, unbothered by the wind. His argument was simple: he did not care who led the Church, but he knew that the keys were in the Quorum of the Twelve and that no man should attempt to come between the Prophet and the Quorum.

Brigham Young was president of the Quorum, and if the keys were with the Twelve, he was now the leader. But it was not the argument itself that moved the people. He spoke with power and feeling, and many of the Saints saw what to them was a miracle. Some reported that he seemed to be transformed into Joseph; even his voice sounded like the voice of the Prophet. They saw in this a symbol that the mantle of authority had fallen upon Brigham Young.

After the speech, the members were asked to vote. Almost unanimously, they voted to sustain the Twelve Apostles as the governing body of the Church, with Brigham Young as the leader.

Sidney Rigdon was not satisfied with this action. He continued to argue for his position and was eventually excommunicated from the Church. A few other persons also claimed leadership, and they drew away some followers. However, these small groups soon died out. Most of the Saints remained loyal to the main body that had accepted the authority of the Quorum of the Twelve.

In the busy days that followed, Brigham Young did not go to visit Emma Smith. They each had strong personalities and had never been close. Emma believed that her eleven-year-old son Joseph III had been ordained by his father to lead the Church. But that claim had not been considered. In the days that followed, she became even more estranged from Brigham Young and his leadership of the Church. She would eventually choose not to follow the Saints to Utah. She remained in Nauvoo and later remarried. In 1860 a new church was formed, known as the Reorganized Church of Jesus Christ of Latter Day Saints. Her son Joseph III became the first president. This church now has its headquarters in Independence, Missouri.

After the Prophet's death, Nauvoo continued to grow and actually come closer to the dream he had envisioned. Log houses were replaced by brick or frame homes with garden plots and neat yards. It was still a backwoods community with muddy streets and lots of wooden sheds and outbuildings, but it was a bustling, active community, rivaling the size of Chicago. Travelers on the Mississippi gathered to the side of riverboats to see the Mormon city with the rising white temple on the bluffs. Many travelers got off the boats to look at the curious people who had built the city, and most were surprised to find a community of industrious, devoted people.

The temple remained the focus of the Saints' commitment. Even as harassment against the Saints began again and the Church's leaders began planning to leave the area, work on the temple continued; in fact, it intensified. Though they were building a temple they would soon aban-

Nauvoo

don to their enemies, the Saints were carrying out the work God had called them to do. In doing so, they were also paying honor to the prophet who had received and announced God's will.

A Seventy's Hall was completed after Joseph's death, and many seventies were called on missions, a special assignment for those who held this calling in the priesthood. A concert hall was also finished, and work on a hotel called the Nauvoo House continued, although the building was never completed.

But all the building could not make the Saints' place in Illinois secure. Their enemies continued to be concerned about the Mormon political power, and their hatred was rekindled. The Nauvoo Charter was repealed by the state legislature, taking away the authority of the courts in the city and dissolving the Nauvoo Legion.

Physical harassment of the Saints began again. Houses were burned in the outlying settlements, and crops were trampled. Brigham Young eventually asked all of the Saints to come to Nauvoo, and he told them that they should take no revenge. Perhaps this would convince the state that the Mormons were peaceable.

All the same, the attacks continued, and newspapers once again called for the Saints to leave the state. But where would they go? Before Joseph's murder, he had spoken of going west to the Rocky Mountains. To Brigham Young, this proposal seemed like a good idea. The Great Salt Lake Valley and surrounding valleys seemed like a place that few others would desire. Perhaps there, in the desert, the Saints would finally be left alone to live and worship as they pleased.

The Saints made plans to leave Illinois in the spring of 1846, once grass on the plains was tall enough to feed the cattle and the rivers were clear of ice. An advance group would push on to the Salt Lake Valley, plant crops, and begin to prepare for the mass migration.

In the meantime, work on the temple in Nauvoo became more intense. Though it was being built at great cost by a people who would soon have to leave their homes, the Saints were willing to make the sacrifice. They knew that it would be some time before other temples could be built, and they wanted and needed the blessings that would come to them through the sacred ceremonies performed there.

Over the next few months, though the temple was not yet completed, more than five thousand Latter-day Saints received instruction in the temple and took solemn vows. They committed themselves fully to the Lord's work, knowing that the Lord would bless and reward them for their righteous efforts.

The Saints planned to leave Nauvoo in the late spring. However, that winter rumors reached them that federal troops were coming to attack the city (the rumors later

The exodus from Nauvoo

turned out to be false), so preparations were increased. In early February wagons carrying the people began to roll across the frozen Mississippi River. Many walked alongside them.

In Iowa, on the western side of the river, the people camped in wagons and tents, subject to the wind and snow. Many were sick, and exposure to the bitter weather soon began to take lives.

Eliza R. Snow wrote: "On the first night of the encampment, nine children were born into the world, and from that time as we journeyed onward mothers gave birth to offspring under almost every variety of circumstances imaginable, except those to which they had been accustomed; some in tents, others in wagons—in rain-storms, and in snow-storms. I heard of one birth which occurred under the rude shelter of a hut, the sides of which were formed of blankets fastened to poles stuck in the ground, with a bark roof through which the rain was dripping; kind sisters stood holding dishes to catch the water as it fell, thus protecting the newcomer and its mother from a shower bath as the little innocent first entered this stage of human life."

The suffering was especially terrible for the children. When they became sick with simple illnesses that would be little problem with modern medicine, they were often doomed. There was no way to control raging fevers, and because they were exposed to the cold, many died and were buried in Iowa.

As they reached the last point from which they could see back across the river, many persons turned to have a last look at their city, which they now called the "City of Joseph" in honor of the martyred prophet. One person described this last lingering look at the temple on the bluffs: "I have no words with which to convey a proper conception of my feelings when taking a last look at this sacred monument of the living faith of the Saints. . . . After the lapse of thirty-six years I can scarcely restrain my feelings when I write it."

Another thought was also common among the Saints. Jane Young, wife of Joseph Young, expressed this thought in her diary. Though she was worried about her children, who cried "much of the time," she vowed: "We are leaving our homes today to cross the frozen river. We must not look back; but placing our faith in God, we must leave our destiny in his hands."

CHAPTER 17

Westward Migration

As spring came on, the Saints began to push across Iowa. Wagons often bogged down in the mud, making progress tediously slow. Supplies were short, but Brigham Young did his best to see that all were cared for. The Saints were organized into companies and leaders were chosen. Many of the organizing patterns were those used in the Zion's Camp march from Kirtland to Missouri many years earlier.

Hosea Stout wrote in his journal almost daily. He described rainstorms that turned the road into heavy mud and changed small streams into threatening rivers. At night, the rains soaked the bedding in the makeshift tents. Later, the heat and dust created new ordeals. Once, when the Stout family's supplies dwindled to nothing, President Young, who traveled back and forth among the Saints along the trail, made certain the Stouts received food to keep them going.

Hosea's diary reveals a people doing their best under stress, sometimes losing their tempers and quarreling. He reports that he was very angry with a brother who had "acted the rascal" and cheated him. He was also upset with one of his leaders who, he felt, was acting unfairly. And yet, he

didn't decide to forget the Saints and look out only for himself. He rose above his personal concerns and sacrificed for
the common cause, as did the other pioneers.

The diary also reveals how often the members of the
camp were sick. Hosea himself suffered with a recurring
fever. His wife had pleurisy and at one point was near death.
Twice he mentioned men in their group who died along the
way, but worst of all was the loss of the children. On Friday,
May 8, 1846, Hosea wrote:

"In the after noon I went out in company with Benjn
Jones into the wood being very lonesome and was talking
over our feelings when I was sent for and informed that my
little son Hyrum was dying. I returned immediately home
and found the poor little afflicted child in the last agonies
of death. He died in my arms about four o'clock. This was
the second child which I had lost both dying in my arms.
He died with hooping cough & black canker. He had worn
down ever since he first took it. . . .

"I shall not attempt to say anything about my feelings at
this time because my family is still afflicted. My wife is yet
unable to go about & little Hosea my only son now is wearing down with the same complaint and what will be the end
thereof. I have fearful foreboding of coming evil on my family yet We are truly desolate of any thing even to eat much
less to nourish the sick & just able to go about my self. Ar-
raingements were made to bury him this evening."

Later in the month Stout wrote that little Hosea was
growing worse, as was his wife. All the same, it was time to
move on. He "repaired" the grave of his son and expected to
"start soon & never see it again." Two days later his wife was
doing better. "It seemed like new life to see her even thus re-
covering from a long sickness," he wrote.

But his son did not get better. A month later, on a Sunday morning, he "seemed to go to sleep," and died without

pain. "Thus died my only son and one too on whom I had placed my own name and was truly the dearest object of my heart." The Stouts now had only their baby still alive, and Hosea feared that she too would be "laid by the way side."

For a moment he allowed himself to express the pain: "This the darling object of my heart gone seemed to cap the climax of all my former misfortunes and seemed more than all else to leave me utterly hopeless. But I shall cease to indulge my feelings any longer."

And that was the end of his self-pity. He praised those who came to his aid. He took one day to "fix up and arrange . . . affairs." The next day he worked on a bridge with the brethren. And a few days later he and his little family were moving on again.

That summer, many of the Saints reached the valley of the Missouri River, the western boundary of Iowa. Many camped in Indian country on both sides of the river. Eventually, the largest body of Saints would gather at a site that

Winter Quarters

came to be known as Winter Quarters, near present-day
Omaha, Nebraska. The plan was that most of the Saints
would stay there for the winter, while an advance group
would push on to the Salt Lake Valley and start to plant
crops and establish an encampment there.

Plans changed, however. First, the ordeal of the Iowa
crossing, with such hasty preparations, had required more
time than expected. Settlements had to be established along
the way, to provide for those who would come after.

As the encampment gradually built up in western Iowa
and Winter Quarters, a new challenge forced adjustments in
the Saints' plans. The United States government sent its
representative, Captain James Allen, to recruit five hundred
Mormon men to fight in the war against Mexico over dis-
puted territory in the southwest. At first, the Saints were
anything but enthusiastic about the idea. After all, this was
the government that had refused to help the Saints earlier in
Missouri and then Illinois. On the Fourth of July Hosea
Stout wrote in his dairy: "Today is our Nation's annaversary
or birth day of her liberty while we are fleeing exiles from her
tyranny and oppression."

But Brigham Young's view was quite different. He saw
the government's request as an opportunity to prove the loyalty of the Saints to the United States and to help win for
the country the very territory that the Saints were moving
to. More immediately, he saw a way to bring in much
needed cash through the pay the recruited soldiers would receive.

President Young was aware, in fact, that the arrangements for the army had been made by members and friends
of the Church for those very reasons. He was soon riding
from one encampment to another, helping with the recruit-
ment. And the skeptical Church members began to sign up
for the march.

On July 20, 541 soldiers, along with about one hundred other Mormons, many of them women and children, began the march to the Mexican war. The unit was called the Mormon Battalion, and its march became the longest in U.S. military history. The Mormon troops—along with a larger non-Mormon force—marched south to Fort Leavenworth, Kansas, and then southwest to the border of Mexico, but by then the war with Mexico was over. They continued on, however, to San Diego, California, where they served as an occupation force.

The battalion fired no bullets and won no war. Their only battle was with a herd of wild bulls. But they crossed a desert, prepared a wagon trail, dug wells, survived an unprecedented ordeal, and marched over two thousand miles. When the troops were mustered out in July 1847, some headed for the Great Salt Lake Valley, where they met the early vanguard of the Saints there. Some then crossed the Rockies and plains again to bring their families to the valley. Others stayed in California for a time to raise money. Several were at Sutter's Fort in northern California when gold was discovered, setting off the gold rush. But most of them left the gold fields and returned to the Salt Lake Valley. The gathering of the Saints was more important to them than the gathering of gold.

Not long after the Mormon Battalion began its march, the final blow was dealt to the few hundred Mormons still in Nauvoo. Most of the Saints had left in the early spring, but some were too sick or old to travel, and others had no means to buy the wagons and food necessary for the exodus. For a time, the citizens of Illinois had let the Mormons go in peace, but when it appeared that some might stay on another winter, harassment began again.

On September 12, mobs from Carthage attacked the Mormons in Nauvoo. A few men were killed on both sides, but the Mormons had no way to defend themselves. The town was plundered, and the last of the loyal Saints were forced to cross the river. Over six hundred made this last crossing, bringing the total of Saints driven out of Illinois to over twelve thousand. But these last persons were the least able to care for themselves because of their poverty and illness.

When word about this "poor camp" reached Church leaders, they sent help, but food and other provisions were still sparse. Then on October 9, flocks of quail began to land all along the Mississippi bottomlands. The birds had become exhausted from long flight, and they were easily caught. This was manna from heaven—a miracle—to the thankful Saints.

It was in that same spirit that William Clayton wrote the words to the best known of Mormon hymns. His wife Diantha had had to remain in Nauvoo, for her baby was due soon. Feeling alone and worried in an Iowa camp one night, he received word that his wife had given birth to a daughter, and both were well. He sat down and wrote these words for a hymn, using music from an old song:

> Come, come, ye Saints, no toil nor labor fear;
> But with joy wend your way.
> Though hard to you this journey may appear,
> Grace shall be as your day.
> 'Tis better far for us to strive
> Our useless cares from us to drive;
> Do this, and joy your hearts will swell—
> All is well! All is well!

The next two verses continued with the hopeful message, and then the final verse proclaimed:

> And should we die before our journey's through,
> Happy day! All is well!
> We then are free from toil and sorrow, too;

With the just we shall dwell!
But if our lives are spared again
To see the Saints their rest obtain,
Oh, how we'll make this chorus swell—
All is well! All is well!

As it turned out, the hymn was prophetic. That year 359
died in the winter camps, and the consolation for the people
was that their loved ones would dwell with the just. But the
Saints were also destined to obtain their rest, or at least
reach their destination and prosper there. Rest would come
only as freedom from violent attacks; toil and labor would be
their lot for the rest of their lives.

All across the nation and the world, the gathering to the
West was taking place. One group of Mormons, led by
Samuel Brannan, left New York on the ship *Brooklyn* to sail
around South America's Cape Horn to San Francisco. From
there they would travel across the Sierras and the deserts of
Nevada and western Utah to the Salt Lake Valley.

Another group, from the state of Mississippi, began their
own trek west, taking a different route than the main body
of the pioneer Saints.

But most of the Saints gathered near Winter Quarters to
await the big migration the next spring. Winter Quarters itself was a sort of miracle—a city built in a matter of weeks,
but sufficient to house the Saints for the winter and to house
others who would come after.

The vanguard company, the first to head west and prepare the way for the others, departed from Winter Quarters
in April 1847, following trails along the Platte River. Led by
Brigham Young, the group included 143 men and 3 women.
Two six-year-old boys, Lorenzo Young's son and stepson,
also made the trip. They had plenty to do, since the company took 93 horses, 52 mules, 66 oxen, 19 cows, 17 dogs,

and some chickens. The boys helped herd and feed animals along the way.

The party traveled in seventy-three wagons and carriages, taking with them a cannon and a leather boat for crossing rivers. Each morning they arose at five, to the sound of a horn. By seven the wagons were underway. Every man was to carry a gun, since no one knew what to expect from Indians. At night they circled the wagons, building fires outside and keeping the horses within the circle. At eight-thirty everyone was to retire to the wagons for prayer, and by nine o'clock all were to be in bed.

Brigham Young, as leader, was never one to understate his thoughts. On one occasion he told the men: "Yester-day there was no one with the cows, and they started twice to go to the Buffalo and I had to run my horse twice to bring them back, in doing which I lost a good telescope. I did not know then that Erastus Snow was the driver for that time. If I had, I should have known that he would not go out of this road one rod, he is so lazy."

Elder Snow did not appreciate the remark, and some harsh words were exchanged. But the brethren knew President Young, and they respected his leadership, even loved him for his straightforward way of speaking. It was a time that demanded strength, and Brigham Young was definitely strong.

Along the way the company met up with the well-known mountain man Jim Bridger. He knew the Great Basin and gave them some encouragement. He especially praised the area around Utah Lake, some thirty miles south of the Great Salt Lake. He was, however, skeptical as to whether corn could be raised in the dry basin. But other travelers they met were more positive, and President Young felt reassured that they had chosen a reasonable destination.

In late June Samuel Brannan met the company. He had

come all the way from San Francisco Bay to encourage the Saints to continue to the West Coast. He had nothing but praise for California. However, President Young knew that California would be an area desired by many others, and he wanted the Saints to settle in an area where they could live and worship in peace. Brannan returned to California and eventually left the Church.

As the pioneer company reached the Rocky Mountains, travel became very difficult. Temperatures were very cold at night and hot during the day. The horses and oxen continually had to struggle up and then down steep hillsides and to ford many rivers and streams. Added to this, some of the men became sick with mountain fever.

On July 12 Brigham fell ill, and for a while the company feared for his life. He was kept behind with some others who were sick. One small group went ahead to scout and prepare the road. The largest group followed, and the detachment of those who were sick trailed behind.

On July 20, 1847, the advance group reached East Canyon, not far from Salt Lake Valley. The next day Orson Pratt and Erastus Snow rode ahead and entered the valley for the first time. They shouted with joy when they saw the Great Salt Lake and the broad valley that would be their home. The advance company then set about to make the canyons passable for the others.

On July 22 the first two companies entered the valley. The next day they pushed the final few miles closer to the Great Salt Lake. Orson Pratt offered a prayer, giving thanks for their arrival and consecrating the land to the Lord. By noon furrows were being plowed and crops planted.

That same day Brigham got his first glimpse of the valley. He said the spirit of light rested on him and that he "felt the Saints would find protection and safety" here. The next day, July 24, he arrived in the valley. It was then that he told Wilford Woodruff, "This is the right place. Drive on."

Some in the company praised the blue skies and the beauty of the valley. Others saw a desert and wondered how a new Zion could be built in such a place. Lorenzo Young said that everything looked "gloomy and I was heartsick." His wife Harriet said, "We have traveled fifteen hundred miles to get here, and I would willingly travel a thousand miles farther" to get to a place where she thought they could live. She saw nothing but barren wasteland.

But Brigham Young had said something earlier that expressed a more prevalent feeling among the Saints: "I could a deal easier saw up this house and eat it for Indian meal and give satisfaction than go over the mountains. . . . I just do the thing that I know to be right and the Lord blesses me."

CHAPTER 18

In the Great Basin

On July 28, 1847, Brigham Young's strength was beginning to return. He went for a walk, looking over the new valley. Suddenly he stopped and waved his arm. "Here is the forty acres for the temple," he said. "The city can be laid out perfectly square, north and south, east and west."

The forty-acre site for the temple was later reduced to ten, but anyone who has ever been to Temple Square in Salt Lake City has seen what President Young envisioned. He was like Joseph Smith in that regard. He looked at what was, but he saw what could be. He was a practical man, able to manage the settlement of a desert valley. And gradually, though very different from Joseph, he was winning the respect and love of the Saints.

The work of preparing the valley for future companies was divided up among the early pioneer company. One group began to explore along the front of the Wasatch Mountains, where most of the good farm land was to be found. Another group began to cut timber in a nearby canyon. The largest group was assigned to build a walled-in fort and log cabins within it.

One small party was assigned to hunt and fish. In the

next eight days they managed to kill "one hare, one badger, one white wolf, and three sage hens," and to catch four fish. They had better luck gathering salt—which was much more plentiful than was the wild game.

A bowery, a shelter that was topped with brush and boughs, was constructed on the temple lot, and here church meetings were held. At the meetings, Brigham Young announced the standards by which he expected the Saints to live. No land would be purchased; rather, each family would be given a plot in the city. But no one would be allowed to divide and sell the lot for profit.

The city would be laid out in blocks, ten acres in size, with eight lots to a block. The streets were to be wide enough for an ox team and wagon to turn around in—eight rods wide. The Saints would plant gardens on their lots, but farming would take place outside the city. Each family received a parcel of land to farm.

President Young's vision was of a people who were self-sustaining, free from the influence of those who had driven

Brigham Young, about 1852

them from their homes in the East and Midwest. While he hoped that the Great Basin area would someday become a state, he saw it as an independent society, operated on the laws of God. Above all, he wanted no trade with the outside world, no dependence on those who might take advantage of the Saints.

Barely a month after President Young's arrival, he was heading back to Winter Quarters with about one hundred men. Those who stayed in the valley were to build and cultivate; those who were returning to Winter Quarters would lead other companies back to this new Zion.

Conditions in the valley that winter were extremely difficult. The Saints had been overly optimistic in sending so many west the first season. Over fifteen hundred arrived, and these were joined by some of the Mormon Battalion men arriving from California. Crops turned out to be inadequate, especially when cattle and horses somehow managed to get into them.

The Saints tried to make the best of things. Under the leadership of the newly organized stake presidency, headed by John Smith, the Prophet Joseph's uncle, cabins were built and the fort was extended. All available food was rationed, but there was often little to eat. Priddy Meeks said that he and his family went several months without a "satisfying meal." But he made do on what he could find.

"I shot hawks and crows and they ate well," he said. "I would go and search the mire holes and find cattle dead and fleece off what meat I could and eat it. We used wolf meat, which I thought was good. I made some wooden spades to dig seagoes [sego lilies] with, but we could not supply our wants. . . . I would take a grubbing hoe and a sack and start by sunrise in the morning and go, I thought six miles before coming to where the thistle roots grew, and in time to get home I would have a bushel and sometimes more thistle roots. And we would eat them raw. I would dig until I grew weak and faint and sit down and eat a root, and then begin again."

Nonetheless, the Saints survived. Now they placed their hopes on the spring harvest. A late frost, however, damaged the crops, and then as sprouts began to grow again, crickets came out of the mountains in hordes. The people fought for their existence, using brooms, shovels, and sacks to smash the huge black insects. But the numbers were too great. The crickets moved across fields like an army, chewing the wheat and vegetable sprouts down to the very ground. One person said the crickets were like a cross between a "spider and a buffalo."

Just as stake leaders began considering another move by the Saints, large flocks of seagulls swooped in from the islands of the Great Salt Lake and began to devour the crickets. They fed until bloated, spat up the indigestible parts, and then ate more. Much of the crop was saved.

For the Mormons this was a miracle, a sign that the Lord was looking out for them in this arid valley. Priddy Meeks wrote that "this circumstance changed our feeling considerable for the better."

All the same, the outlook was not good. Many believed they should push on to California, where the climate was better. The growing season was too short in this valley, and rain seldom fell. Life here would mean scratching for an existence, laboring to dam up creeks for irrigation and hauling timber out of the mountains, always storing for the long winters.

Some did move on. Others made the long trip back to the Midwest. But most stayed, not because they liked the place, but because a prophet had guided them there.

By spring that prophet was leading more Mormon refugees to the Salt Lake Valley. It was a huge company: 397

wagons, 1,229 people, 74 horses, 1,275 oxen, 699 cows, 184 loose cattle, 411 sheep, 141 pigs, 605 chickens, 37 cats, 82 dogs, 3 goats, 10 geese, 2 beehives, 8 doves, and 1 crow.

For three and a half years Brigham Young had led the Church as the senior member of the Quorum of the Twelve Apostles. Now, in Winter Quarters, he was sustained as President of the Church, with Heber C. Kimball and Willard Richards as his counselors.

As a leader, he was sometimes quick to call the Saints to repentance, and he occasionally lost his temper. But he could also be tender. He was close to the people, intimately concerned with their personal problems. Along the trail to the valley he would stroll through the camps in the evenings and chat with the Saints.

On one occasion a woman in the company, Lucy Groves, slipped under a wagon and broke her leg. She had given birth to a baby just ten days before. The leg was set but then was rebroken in another accident. Lucy was miserable, the bumping of the wagon causing more pain than she could tolerate. Her husband decided to turn the wagon out and let the others move on.

But President Young would not allow that. Earlier he had set Lucy's broken bone himself; now he cut the legs from her bed and suspended the bed from ropes in the wagon. This stopped the bumping. He blessed Lucy and promised her that she would reach the valley and live many years. Then he rode alongside her wagon for several days. Lucy's grandson wrote, "With his gentle kind manner, he won the love of Lucy and her posterity forever."

On the other hand, when some of the men shot buffalo along the way, just for the sport of it, President Young didn't worry about the sharpness of his tongue in calling them to repentance. And when he met two families along the trail who had given up on the Great Basin and were heading back to civilization, he spared no words. He told them never to return to the valley until they were ready to be "Saints indeed," and he promised to blot their names "out of remembrance." Then he gave them twenty-five pounds of meal, to make certain they had enough to make their journey.

As the summer came on, grass was scarce along the trail, as was wood for burning. The animals suffered. Hosea Stout recorded in his journal: "One ox of John Alger melted and died." The women burned "buffalo chips"—dried buffalo dung—and cooked meals over them. Clean water was so scarce that a new well had to be dug almost every day.

Though travel along the trail was difficult, the Saints relaxed each evening with dances, comical readings, and musical performances. No one loved music and fun more than Brigham Young. It was a way of making the best of the situation, a needed relief. As one man wrote: "We are as comfortable and happy as most of the stationary communities. For if we have not all that our wants may call for, we have the art of lessening our wants, which does as well."

Not all the Saints were "saintly" all the time, but the overall unity and behavior of a people who had been through so much was remarkable. As they neared their destination, they gathered their companies together and allowed President Young's group to come to the front. Then they entered the valley as a huge train. The settlers who had survived the winter came out in great numbers to greet them and to celebrate.

Just as the advance party had done the year before, the new arrivals organized quickly and began to build. Lots were assigned to them, and the city was divided into wards, with bishops called to lead in each. Members of the First Presidency and the Quorum of Twelve Apostles were assigned parcels of land near the temple site. Brigham Young soon built a whole row of log houses, into which moved his wives and families.

Preparations for the winter of 1848-49 were better, but

the harvest had been less than adequate. Added to that, the winter was more harsh than the winter before. Cattle died in great numbers, and the people, crowded into adobe homes, suffered from the lack of food. Some even boiled rawhide to make "glue soup." Harvesting roots was difficult in the frozen ground. If the first year had been a trial, the second brought the Saints to the brink of disaster.

And then word began to spread that gold had been discovered in California. The temptation to move on to a place where wealth could be picked up off the ground, where the climate was mild and the soil rich, was almost too much for many of the people.

But President Young held his ground. He told his followers: "We have been kicked out of the frying-pan into the fire, out of the fire into the middle of the floor, and here we will stay. God . . . will temper the elements for the good of his Saints; He will rebuke the frost and the sterility of the soil, and the land shall become fruitful. . . . Let others seek [gold], and we will cultivate the soil. . . . Plow your land and sow wheat, plant your potatoes."

What followed that summer of 1849 was a rich harvest—but not just of the crops. Perhaps no one benefited more from the gold rush than did the Mormons.

When word of the discovery of gold reached the East Coast, many trading companies tried to get goods to California, hoping for big sales. But those that traveled overland were beaten by those that went around Cape Horn with ships. Rather than continue to California, they let everything go at rock-bottom prices in the Salt Lake Valley. Prospective miners rushing to the gold fields also grew impatient by the time they reached Great Salt Lake Valley. They would sell almost everything they had, dirt cheap, just to get hold of a good horse for quick travel.

The Mormons were able to sell their crops for very high

prices, and they bought goods for almost nothing. They had desperately needed clothing, iron to make tools, and household goods; now such items came to them like an overflow from heaven. Mormon companies heading for the valley also picked up abandoned goods strewn along the trail— tools, grain, stoves, anything heavy. The emigrants to California were lightening their wagons to get to the gold.

Most of the forty-niners made little gain from their rush to the West Coast. But the Mormons, who might otherwise have had to struggle for years to furnish their homes and get established in the Salt Lake Valley, suddenly possessed most of the things they desired.

CHAPTER 19

The State of Deseret

In 1849 the pioneer Saints celebrated both the fourth and the twenty-fourth of July. One was the birthday of the country they still considered themselves part of; the other was the anniversary of their arrival in the Great Salt Lake Valley. Both celebrations were marked by a show of American patriotism, despite some bitter feelings the Saints had had in the past.

For a while, Church and government in the valley meshed together entirely. Brigham Young led the people in every way. At Church meetings he would often combine advice on irrigation or Indian relations with discourses on man's relation to God. The apostles, stake leaders, and bishops directed every facet of life, from farming to missionary service. When a Church member had a complaint against another, a bishop's court settled the issue. President Young often received requests to settle matters that were personal, not religious. But he handled these with concern, sometimes with humor, and sometimes with his sharp tongue.

The Saints established a provisional government in 1849 and applied for statehood for their State of Deseret. Deseret, a word taken from the Book of Mormon, referred to a hive of bees, a symbol of industry and cooperation. The boundaries of the state extended from the Rockies to the Sierras, including all of present-day Utah and Nevada, a large part of California, almost a third of Arizona, and parts of New Mexico, Colorado, Wyoming, Idaho, and Oregon.

In 1850, when the issue of statehood came to the Congress of the United States, a major concern was slavery. Through a compromise approved by Congress, California, a non-slave territory, was allowed to become a state, while New Mexico and Deseret, renamed Utah, were made territories and allowed to decide for themselves about slavery. The size of Utah was also trimmed.

As a territory, Utah had no vote in Congress. A non-voting representative and territorial officers were appointed rather than elected. Friends in Washington, however, convinced President Millard Fillmore to appoint Brigham Young as governor. The President also appointed some non-Mormons to territorial positions, but it was over a year before they arrived in the valley. In the meantime, the Church and government continued to operate almost as one.

When the non-Mormon judges and appointed officials arrived in 1851, they were not pleased by what they saw. To them, President Young seemed like a dictator. His abrupt and self-assured manner convinced them that they would be ignored. They soon returned to the East.

At the time, President Young was just as happy to see them go. He had viewed them as a nuisance. He had allowed Judge Perry Brocchus an opportunity to speak to the Saints. Judge Brocchus had claimed that the federal government was no enemy of the Saints, but he accused the Mormons of hostility against the country. Then he implied that women members of the Church were not virtuous—probably a reference to plural marriage. The audience was outraged.

Such men were not missed, but their reports to President Fillmore provided the beginnings for suspicion against the Church that would persist in Washington for many years.

For the present, however, the Saints had greater concerns. Brigham Young hoped to settle every desirable location in the territory, and in this way discourage outsiders from settling there. As emigration continued, not only from the Midwest but from Europe, arriving members were wintered in Salt Lake City, but the next spring they were often sent with companies to settle new regions. At first the area along the Wasatch Mountains, which formed the eastern border of the valley, was the focus of settlement. But President Young's plan was to move southward all the way to Southern California and to establish an outpost on the coast to which immigrants could come by sea.

It was not uncommon for one of the Saints, while seated in church, to receive a call to serve a mission. The mission might be one of proselyting, or it might be to settle a town, or it might even be to open a mine or begin some other industry.

Robert Gardner, a sawmill operator, heard one day that he had been volunteered to move to southern Utah to help establish the cotton industry. Having worked hard to establish a home in the Salt Lake Valley, he was not enthusiastic about starting all over on a "cotton mission." He spoke to Elder George A. Smith about it and learned that he was, indeed, on the list.

"I looked and spat, took off my hat, scratched my head, thought and said, 'All right,'" said Gardner.

"Don't blame anyone but me," the apostle told him. "The president asked me to get a list of names for this mission, so I thought of you for one, and thought you would be willing to go, if called; so I put your name down. If you don't want to go, step into the president's office and ask him to take your name off the list, and he will do it."

"I expect he would, but I shan't try him," Gardner concluded. "I have come out to find out what kind of an outfit is wanted, and when we go."

This was the kind of commitment needed to establish the kingdom President Young envisioned. He hoped to create local sources for raw materials and to lessen the Saints' dependence on outside trade. Attempts by the Saints at business enterprises sometimes met with failure or limited success. They experimented with cotton, sugar beets, iron, lead, and woolen goods. Some succeeded, but others failed.

Life in the valley gradually became quite tolerable. Good crops followed the meager ones of the first two years. And as the Saints built homes and planted gardens, the Mormon dream of living in peace as brothers and sisters seemed a real possibility. Idealism ran high. What appeared to outsiders as intrusion into personal affairs by Church leaders did not seem so to the Mormons. That is not to say that they always served without a murmur, or that hard feelings never arose, or even that they always answered the call. But most were willing to serve as called, in spite of reservations they felt at times.

Salt Lake City gradually took on the appearance of an established community. A magnificent temple was planned, but in the meantime an endowment house was built, where temple ordinances could be performed. A social hall became the center for dramatic performances, dances, and other entertainments. Combination church and school buildings were being built throughout the wards.

Much of the construction of public buildings was done by new immigrants. They needed work as they arrived, and so the work was created. A wall was built around the temple site long before the temple was constructed. The primary purpose was to provide work and income for new arrivals rather than to insult their pride with handouts.

Socials were held often in the wards, and the Saints

Salt Lake City, about 1853

found pleasure in dancing or attending plays and musical performances. The Nauvoo Brass Band was revitalized, and the Saints enjoyed any excuse for a parade, a picnic, or a celebration. If the Saints were going to make the desert "blossom as a rose," they had to find joy in their daily lives, and this they always seemed able to do.

By 1852 Brigham Young and the Saints announced publicly that plural marriage was a sanctioned practice of the Church. Only a small minority of the Saints actually ever practiced it, and those who did were often specifically asked to do so.

Plural marriage was not an easy principle to live, but many families lived with it quite comfortably. Wives often had separate houses, each with her own family, but sometimes two or more wives lived in the same home, where they shared the work. Many of the wives became as dear sisters.

Needless to say, any marriage is a challenge to both partners, and in plural marriage the challenges were multiplied. But so long as the Saints were left alone, without the censure of disapproving outsiders, many of the plural marriages were amazingly successful.

Most of the plural marriages involved just two wives. Brigham Young's family was an exception. No one is certain exactly how many women he eventually married. He was married to certain women—such as some who had been sealed to Joseph Smith—only to give them protection and support. He was also sealed to some women who never lived with him. Since the Saints believed that marriage was eternal, some of these marriages were intended to give the woman a husband in the next life, where no eternal mate would otherwise have existed.

All the same, Brigham Young was father to fifty-eight children, borne by sixteen wives. Eleven of the children died in infancy or childhood. Stories and folklore abound about how he managed all his children, but one image comes through all of them. He was strict, with definite rules, but he was also caring and loving. He usually followed his own child-rearing advice:

"Never allow yourselves to become out of temper and get fretful. Why, mother says, 'This is a very mischievous little boy or little girl.' What do you see? That amount of vitality in those little children that they cannot be still. . . . They are so full of life . . . that their bones fairly ache with strength . . . and activity. . . . Do not be out of temper yourselves. Always sympathize with them and soothe them. Be mild and pleasant."

That is not to say that President Young was submissive with his children. On one occasion he came home to find several of his daughters entertaining their boyfriends in the parlor on a Sunday evening. They had stacked up books around a lamp to dim the light. He stepped into the parlor, looked around, and then announced: "The girls will go upstairs to their rooms, and I will say good night to the young men."

In 1854, he built a beautiful home, which became known as the Beehive House because of a beehive-shaped cupola on

Eagle Gate, the entrance to Brigham Young's estate

the roof. This was the place where, as Governor and Church President, he met with the public and held entertainments. Two years later, a large home was built adjacent to the Beehive House, with an office connecting the two structures. The new house, known as the Lion House, was home to several of his wives and their children. Like Joseph Smith, President Young often invited in persons who needed a home. He taught English to many young immigrants by having them work for him, and he paid the educational expenses of many talented young people.

President Young enjoyed having all the family living in the two houses get together in the evenings. He would call on children to perform musical numbers, recite poetry, or perform skits. Popcorn and molasses candy were common treats. After the entertainment, he would read from the scriptures. Always the preacher, he would teach the doctrines of the gospel and admonish the children to live righteously.

In the back part of the house was a family store, where a variety of goods was available. The wives could use their charge accounts to purchase needed items. Other buildings on the property included a blacksmith shop, a carpenter shop, a laundry house, a pigeon house, a shoe shop, a flour mill, barns, corrals, a garden, an orchard, beehives, and patches of berry bushes.

During these early years in the valley, the Church continued to grow. Missionaries were sent to Chile in South America and to China, India, and the islands of the Pacific, but with relatively little success. However, in Europe, especially England and the Scandinavian countries, thousands were joining the Church, and many of these were immigrating to Utah. Most landed in New Orleans and traveled by riverboat up the Mississippi and Missouri rivers, then traveled across the plains in wagons.

A fund known as the Perpetual Emigrating Fund was established to help poor immigrants make the difficult journey. Money was lent to them with the understanding that they would repay, after a reasonable time, to help keep the fund operating. Many remained quite poor, however, and repayment was not always possible.

Because of the financial burden in immigrating, and to save time, an experiment was tried in the late 1850s. Several thousand Saints walked the twelve hundred miles from the Mississippi River, pulling and pushing handcarts. They could bring only minimal provisions, and the march was a weary one, but several thousand made the trek to Utah this way.

In the first year of the experiment, 1856, three companies successfully completed the journey. Two others, known as the Willie and Martin companies, were delayed in starting the trip and didn't set out until late in the season. They were caught by an early snowstorm, and of the thousand people in the companies, approximately 250 died. Others suffered from frostbite, malnutrition, and exposure.

Word of the tragedy reached Brigham Young just as a conference of the Church was to be held. He announced to the congregation: "Many of our brethren and sisters are on the plains with handcarts, and probably many are now seven hundred miles from this place. They must be brought here, we must send assistance to them. . . . I want the brethren who may speak to understand that their text is the people on the Plains. And the subject matter for this community is to send for them and bring them in before the winter sets in. That is my religion; that is the dictation of the Holy Ghost that I possess. It is to save the people."

Few statements by Brigham Young better express his view of a religion of action. Wagons departed immediately, and many lives were saved, but the suffering was not over. Those who wrote of their experiences in the handcart companies left to modern Mormons a monumental example of perseverance in the face of great hardship.

Patience Loader, for example, saw her father die on the trek, but she carried on with her mother, three sisters, and two brothers. She tells of wading through an icy river and then trudging on as her clothing froze to her; of struggling to open a frozen tent and then being unable to drive the stakes into the ground; of rationing food, one quarter pound of flour per person per day; of seeing an eleven-year-old boy crawl to the "sick wagon," his feet frozen and bleeding and his little brother crying by his side; of being ashamed when she faced another frigid river to cross and couldn't hold back the tears.

Then she described her gratitude when three brethren spent the day carrying the weakened pioneers across a frigid stream. Help had come. She wrote: "From this time we began to get more to eat and some shoes and warm under clothing which we all needed verry much. . . . I was thankfull to get a nice warm quilted hood which was very warm and comfortable. I also got apar [a pair] of slippers as I was nearly bear foot. We still had to pull our handcart for atime as there was not wagons suficiant for all to ride."

Finally Patience was able to ride in a wagon, and she made it safely to the Salt Lake Valley. Some of the handcart pioneers brought the bodies of their babies with them, to be buried properly. Most of the dead had to be left behind.

Thirteen-year-old Mary Goble Pay described their arrival in the valley: "Early next morning Bro. Brigham Young and a doctor came. . . . When Bro. Young came in he shook hands with us all. When he saw our condition—our feet frozen and our mother dead—tears rolled down his cheeks. The doctor amputated my toes using a saw and a butcher knife. Brigham Young promised me I would not have to have any more of my feet cut off. The sisters were dressing mother for the last time. Oh how did we stand it? That afternoon she was buried."

But the Saints had endured much suffering before, and they were able to endure this. They passed their commitment and strength on to their children, and the tragedy of the Martin and Willie companies became a testimony to the courage and purpose of a believing people.

The disaster did not stop the march to Zion. Thousands of immigrants continued to come by handcart as well as in wagon trains. By 1856, 40,000 Saints lived in Utah, and thousands more arrived each year thereafter. The Church, which had been driven from one place to another and had been pronounced dead several times, was now established as never before. Dozens of towns had been founded, and the new Kingdom of God was finally taking shape—even if it was a kingdom where people scratched their living from an arid desert, lived in adobe homes, and tried to make the best of a place no one else wanted.

CHAPTER 20

Growth and Opposition

The Mormons had left the settled portions of the United States because they wanted to live their religion in peace. All the same, they hoped the Territory of Utah would become a state. One of the difficulties in obtaining statehood was that federal representatives reported to Washington that the Mormons were governing the territory through the Church. But a more crucial issue was polygamy. To the Mormons, plural marriage was a commandment from God. But non-Mormons opposed the practice strongly. They believed it was wrong to have more than one wife.

In 1854 the Republican Party came into being. In national elections two years later, the party's platform denounced the "twin relics of barbarism": slavery and polygamy. Not only was statehood denied, but legislation and other pressures were used to punish the Saints for polygamy.

Eastern newspapers portrayed Mormon women as degraded, subjected against their wills to a practice they hated. Actually, most plural wives supported the doctrine, believing that they had been called to serve in a special kind of family. On several occasions, after the pressure against polygamy increased, Mormon women held mass rallies and signed petitions to express their support of the principle.

When James Buchanan took office as U.S. President in 1857, he felt compelled to prove that he was opposed to Mormon practices. He appointed Alfred Cumming, a non-Mormon, to be governor of the Utah territory, replacing Brigham Young. Some government officials said that the Mormons would resist this move, and so President Buchanan raised an army to enforce the change.

When Brigham Young learned that the army was on its way, he feared the worst. The Saints had been driven out of too many areas, and he had heard too many assurances that the militias in Missouri and Illinois were peaceful. Joseph Smith had been murdered immediately after such reassurances.

President Young was not going to be caught defenseless. He called the Saints home from missions and from outlying settlements. If necessary, he said, the people should burn their houses and leave a scorched desert for the army to occupy, but he would not submit to murder and harassment.

The government's intentions were not so violent as the Mormons assumed, but fear created an atmosphere of outrage and suspicion in the territory. When a group of emigrants from Arkansas and Missouri, known as the Fancher company, passed through Utah en route to California, word spread that they were insulting Mormons at every opportunity and threatening to do much more. The "Missouri Wildcats," one group within the company, bragged that they had taken part in the attacks on the Saints in Missouri.

The Mormons had been saving food because they were expecting to be attacked by President Buchanan's army. When they refused to sell provisions to the emigrants, the emigrants began to take what they wanted by force.

The Fancher company also angered local Indians, who

claimed that the emigrants had poisoned a spring, killing cattle. The Indians had eaten the meat from the cattle, and some of them died. While the emigrants were camped at Mountain Meadows in southern Utah, the Indians attacked and then held the emigrants under siege for several days. No one knows what all the motivations were, but some of the Mormons in the area joined the Indians in their attack. Brigham Young sent word that the Fancher company should be allowed to move on, but by the time the message was received, it was too late. A bloody massacre had been carried out, killing all but the younger children in the company.

The massacre was passed off as an Indian action for some time, but eventually President Young learned the truth— that some of the Saints had also participated in the massacre. The nation would come to interpret the tragedy as an action by all Mormons and proof that the Saints were taking the law into their own hands.

However, the Saints saw themselves as the ones under attack. Without investigation, President Buchanan had mustered an army to put down a rebellion that never existed. The Saints were not about to enter into warfare with the United States, but they were also not going to sit by and let an army march into the valley and destroy them.

Lot Smith was appointed to lead a band of raiders whose job was to drive off cattle, disrupt travel, burn grass—or do whatever was necessary to delay the troops. On one occasion, he and his men rode into an army camp, convinced the soldiers that he had a larger group than he really had, and set fire to supply wagons. Such actions greatly slowed the army's progress.

Meanwhile, the Mormons were preparing blockades and loosening rocks in the canyons, ready to close off access to the Salt Lake Valley. But the army failed to get that far before winter set in. And when General Johnston, leader of the army, decided to winter in Wyoming at Fort Bridger, which was now owned by the Mormons, he found that the Mormons had burned their own outpost, leaving no buildings for the army to occupy.

Johnston's army set up camp within the walls of the fort and established nearby Camp Scott. There they suffered a hard winter with dwindling supplies. Also during that winter, negotiations had begun with the Saints to settle the misunderstanding. Thomas Kane, a longtime friend of the Mormons, offered to go to Utah to assure Brigham Young that the army was not bent on destroying the Saints.

President Young remained skeptical. Colonel Kane traveled back and forth between Fort Bridger and Salt Lake City, despite ill health and bad weather. He eventually brought the newly appointed governor to Salt Lake City. Governor Cumming was amazed at the gracious treatment and acceptance he was given. He tried to convince the Saints that while the army would march into the valley in the spring, no violent action would be taken.

President Young agreed to let the army come, but the Mormons continued to prepare to leave their homes and flee, if necessary. They were fully prepared to burn every building in Salt Lake City and leave nothing for the army. Some of them even moved to central Utah, to avoid the destruction.

As it turned out, while feelings were anything but kindly between the two groups, no guns were ever fired. Gradually the Saints who had left the city were instructed to return home. Numerous incidents did create bad feelings between the soldiers and the Saints, and the army set up camp in a desolate area west of Utah Lake, but after three years it was withdrawn.

Although the Saints accepted Governor Cumming with little enthusiasm, he turned out to be fair-minded, and he and Brigham Young developed a healthy respect for each other. The Saints were pardoned by President Buchanan, though this hardly softened their feelings, for they felt they had done nothing wrong. But it was the President who ended up looking foolish for wasting so much money to march an army to a war that didn't exist.

The so-called "Mormon War," or "Buchanan's Blunder," also cost the Saints heavily. It had disrupted life—and farming. Missionary work had been stopped, and so had mining and industrial projects. The economy, already struggling, was thrown into depression.

The American Civil War soon turned the nation's attention away from the "Mormon question." President Buchanan's successor, Abraham Lincoln, was less hostile toward the Saints than many politicians. He said that as a boy on the farm he learned that a log was sometimes "too hard to split, too wet to burn, and too heavy to move," and so he plowed around it. The Mormons were like that log. "You go back and tell Brigham Young that if he will let me alone I will let him alone."

All the same, in 1862 President Lincoln signed the Morrill Anti-Bigamy Act. The bill made polygamy a crime and also attacked the Church directly by limiting the amount of property it could hold. The legislation lacked powers of enforcement, however, and President Lincoln did nothing to apply pressure to the Saints.

When the Civil War came to an end in 1865, many Church activities could be resumed. Immigration from Europe increased to pre-war levels, and missionaries were sent to many new parts of the world. Work on the temple in Salt Lake resumed, and many other public works projects were begun, including a large meetinghouse, called a tabernacle, to replace a smaller one built earlier.

As cities built up in the Great Basin, Brigham Young became increasingly concerned about the way too many of the

Salt Lake City (looking south), about 1877

Mormons were beginning to live. In his travels throughout the territory, his message was increasingly the return to basic values. To protect the economy, he told the Saints to boycott non-Mormon merchants. He advised communities to set up cooperative businesses from which every citizen received some economic benefit, to keep the profits from returning to the East. He established Zion's Cooperative Mercantile Institution (ZCMI), at first a wholesale outlet and later a retail business. He saw in such cooperative efforts a way to avoid the problem of a few getting rich at the expense of all others.

President Young also strongly urged the Mormons to resist certain sins of the world. He did not discourage wholesome enjoyments. He was extremely proud, for instance, of the beautiful Salt Lake Theater, which the Saints had built. He supported the theater, attended often, and encouraged his daughters to participate as actresses. But what he detested was the snobbishness of those who showed up at public events in fancy clothing and ornaments.

He saw young men go on missions and gain the faith and

strength of purpose they needed, but he feared that young women were given to "silly, extravagant speeches and light-mindedness of thought." Thus, he encouraged a young women's "retrenchment" society—a sort of back-to-basics movement. The organization, which later became the Young Women's Improvement Association, was formed in 1869 and soon spread throughout the Church. A few years later, a similar organization was formed for the young men.

The early leaders of the young women's organization were President Young's daughters. They resolved to "discard . . . dragging skirts, and for decency's sake those disgustingly short ones extending no lower than the boot tops." They also agreed "as fast as it shall be expedient" to adopt the wearing of homemade articles. And, more importantly, they resolved to store their minds with "useful knowledge" and to prepare to fill "honorable and useful positions in the Kingdom of God."

Contrary to the view of many men of the time, President Young did not believe that women were merely decorative objects. He told the Saints, "We believe that women are useful, not only to sweep houses, wash dishes, make beds, and raise babies, but that they should stand behind the counter, study law or physic [medicine], or become good bookkeepers and be able to do the business in any counting house, and all this to enlarge their sphere of usefulness for the benefit of society at large. In following these things they but answer the design of their creation."

The Women's Relief Society, which had begun in Nauvoo in 1842, was reestablished in Utah under the direction of Eliza R. Snow. Through this organization and its publications, women's voices were heard throughout the territory. Women in the territory were the first in the nation to receive the vote. The *Woman's Exponent,* a publication for Mormon women, became a voice for women's rights.

The Relief Society gradually became a great force for

good throughout the Church. Along with teaching house-hold skills, child care, and the doctrines of the gospel, the women operated granaries and storage facilities to provide a ready supply of food and staples for the needy. They raised silkworms in an attempt to establish a home-based profit-making industry. They participated in several national women's movements and supported the peace movement of the day. They were also prominent in the suffrage move-ment, campaigning for women's right to vote.

A number of Mormon women were sent to the East to study. Ellis Reynolds Shipp was sponsored by Brigham Young himself. She left her family, as missionaries did, and studied medicine in Philadelphia. She became a prominent obstetrician in Utah and a leader in the National Council of Women. At the same time she continued to bear and rear children and to serve in Church and civic organizations.

President Young was also concerned that many Saints were ignoring the Word of Wisdom—the health law Joseph Smith had received by revelation—not thinking of it as the will of the Lord but only as good advice. While few Mor-mons drank hard liquor or smoked, many drank wine, cof-fee, and tea, and many men chewed tobacco. It was time for this to change, and increased emphasis on the law was given in sermons and articles. Not only would health be im-proved, but it would no longer be necessary to import such items, and the money saved could be contributed to help the poor gather to the valley. Most important, President Young wanted to see the Saints brought closer to the Lord by com-plying with all his revelations.

President Young also turned his attention to education of the Saints. He reopened the School of the Prophets, al-though in a new form. He gathered leaders of the Church and their wives to instruct them on the deeper meanings of the gospel. He also supported the creation of a Sunday School, which at first was an organization only for children.

Brigham Young, about 1877

As to public schools, he supported the establishment of academies, which eventually became Utah's colleges and universities, and he encouraged improvements in elementary schools. The difficult early years in the valley had required that emphasis be placed on the practical need for survival. Education of children, while not ignored, had not been given adequate attention. Now schools were begun through ward organizations.

In President Young's last years, he pushed hard for the highest expression of what he believed: cooperative communities where no one would be rich and no one would be poor, communities where the Saints would live together in harmony and be committed to the prosperity of all. During his last years, he traveled throughout the territory to set up such systems. Brigham Young, in his usual original and visionary way, saw the possibility of raising the Saints to a new and finer level of Christian living, a way to raise a whole society to economic well-being.

President Young died in 1877, apparently of a ruptured appendix. He was seventy-six years old. At the last moment, he opened his eyes, looked toward a window, and said, "Joseph! Joseph! Joseph!" Those in the room felt certain that he was seeing the Prophet, Joseph Smith. Over the next few days tens of thousands came to the Tabernacle to pay their last respects to their beloved leader, the colonizer and prophet, Brigham Young.

SECTION V

THE WORLDWIDE CHURCH

At the time of Brigham Young's death, most people in America thought of Mormons as a somewhat strange little group in the Mountain West. While the Saints were fairly well-known in northern Europe, a great percentage of the world had barely heard of the Church's existence. Who would have predicted the growth the next hundred years would bring?

The Saints would have predicted it. Joseph Smith had done so long ago, and the faith of the Saints had always been that the Church would "roll forth" to all the world. But even to the faithful, the rate of growth has been startling—a modern miracle. It was a movement that began with miracles, and so it has continued.

CHAPTER 21

The Manifesto

John Taylor, as president of the Quorum of the Twelve Apostles, took over the leadership of the Church when Brigham Young died. Once again, for a period of about three years, no President was sustained. Elder Taylor led as the head of the governing quorum. Finally, in October 1880, he was sustained by the membership as the President, Prophet, Seer, and Revelator.

As a young man, President Taylor had been a Methodist minister in Canada. He was converted to Mormonism by Parley P. Pratt in 1836. He served as a great missionary in England, and was in Carthage Jail with Joseph and Hyrum Smith on the afternoon they were murdered. No one was more committed than he to the principles of the gospel.

John Taylor was a man very different from either Joseph Smith or Brigham Young. He did not have the youthful intensity of Joseph nor the assertive power of Brigham, but he was a strong leader, firm and farsighted. A tall man, he dressed neatly and was always well-groomed. President Young had sometimes jokingly, if not tactfully, called him "Prince John."

"Prince" may have applied to his appearance, but not to

John Taylor

his attitude toward people. When the apostles suggested that he move into the elaborate Gardo House, he refused several times. This mansion had been started under Brigham Young's direction and was to serve as the living quarters for future Presidents. President Taylor eventually did move in, but he did not like to live in elegance. His tastes were simple, and he disliked anything that would seem to set him off from the Saints.

The fiftieth anniversary of the Church was observed in 1880. At April conference that year, President Taylor explained that in Hebrew tradition, this was the year of jubilee, or celebration. He followed the Hebrew tradition by making several proposals to ease the burden of the poor. The indebtedness of immigrants who were still very poor would be forgiven, as would half of all back tithing. A thousand cattle and five thousand sheep would be given to needy families. In addition, the Relief Society was asked to lend wheat to farmers who had suffered a bad harvest the previous fall.

After the Saints voted to accept the proposal, President Taylor pronounced, "It is the time of Jubilee!" He then asked the members to be generous. The wealthy should be quick to forgive the debts of those who were struggling to survive. "Free the worthy, debt-bound brother if you can. Let there be no rich among us from whose tables fall crumbs to feed a wounded Lazarus," he said.

This was, in President Taylor's way, a commitment to the principles the first two prophets had taught. Both Joseph Smith and Brigham Young had tried at times to set up societies based on cooperation and brotherly love. But these experiments were not going well; one after another, they were discontinued. All the same, President Taylor never wanted to see the day when brother would be set against brother for the sake of material gain. The Saints had come to the valleys of the West to establish something better than that.

The next few years continued to be years of growth for the Church. Attempts were made to establish the gospel in Mexico, South America, New Zealand, Turkey, and Palestine. All of these missions met with relatively little success, but the missions in the United States and in Europe continued to bring in many converts, and immigration to Utah went on at a steady pace.

President Taylor continued to establish settlements throughout the territory as well as in Wyoming, Nevada, and Arizona. Many Saints who were established in and around Salt Lake City had no desire to start over in a new settlement. But if their skills were needed, they were sometimes called to go with new immigrants to establish communities in other locations. Rarely did anyone refuse such a call.

As opposition to plural marriage increased, some of the

Saints were sent to establish a colony in northern Mexico, where the government did nothing to stop the practice. Eventually over three thousand members lived in Colonia Juarez and the surrounding area. There they suffered great hardships in settling such a rugged desert area. In 1912, when the Mexican Revolution began, most of the Saints returned to the United States. A few later returned to the colonies, but Church direction of the programs there was carried out from mission leaders in California.

Other Mormons were sent to Canada, where they settled in southern Alberta. Those settlements prospered and grew, and a large Mormon population continues today to live in that area.

During his administration, President Taylor oversaw the preparation of a new edition of the Doctrine and Covenants, with 136 sections. An edition of Joseph Smith's writings, including his personal history and his translations of ancient papyrus, was issued in 1880. Titled the Pearl of Great Price, this book had first been published in England in 1851, but now, with some modifications, it became one of the Mormon standard works of scripture, along with the Bible, the Book of Mormon, and the Doctrine and Covenants.

In 1878, Aurelia Rogers formed an organization for children in Farmington, Utah. The organization, which became known as the Primary Association, was designed to teach children about the gospel and to combine entertaining and useful training in crafts and arts. It also sponsored fife and drum bands, which became quite popular. The Primary program spread and gradually took its place as one of the Church auxiliaries, along with Young Men's and Young Women's MIA organizations, the Relief Society, and the Sunday School.

Since the time of the first antipolygamy legislation, pressure from Washington for the Saints to stop the practice gradually increased. For some time they had held out hope that laws against plural marriage would be ruled unconstitutional. In 1879, however, the Church received a decision on a test case and lost. To test the law, George Reynolds voluntarily admitted that he had more than one wife. He justified his marital practice on religious grounds. After a series of trials and appeals, the Supreme Court upheld his conviction.

This was only the first of many decisions to go against the Church. In 1882 the Edmunds Act was passed by Congress, making "cohabitation," or the continuation of existing plural marriages, illegal. Fines and jail terms were prescribed, and anyone involved in plural marriage was to be barred from serving in territorial government offices.

The Mormons were caught in a difficult dilemma. They believed in obeying the law of the land, and they hoped to be accepted as a state of the United States. But they also believed that the principle of plural marriage was God's will. When Rudger Clawson, the first person to be prosecuted under the new law, stood before Judge Zane, he said, "Your honor, I very much regret that the laws of my country should come in conflict with the laws of God; but whenever they do, I shall invariably choose the latter."

The judge was not moved by the argument, nor was anyone in Washington. Over the next several years hundreds of Mormon men went to jail. Every legal attempt by the Saints to fight the crusade against them failed. In one case the courts even ruled that a man was guilty even if he no longer lived with a second wife but continued to supply her and her children with food and shelter. In other words, the Saints were being asked not only to give up their beliefs to avoid jail, but also to abandon their families. This they were not willing to do.

Many Mormon men went "underground," hiding from law enforcement officers to avoid arrest. Federal agents combed the territory, hunting down known polygamists, watching their homes, and raiding suspected hideouts.

The pressure on polygamist families was intense. Nancy Williams, in order to protect her husband, Frederick, from prosecution, had to pretend that she was not married. Once, after not seeing him for a month, she saw his wagon in town. She wrote in her diary: "I went to the Post office, then to the store, in hopes of seeing him. He passed the store while I was there with a load of coal, on his way to Manti. He nodded, and I returned it. And went home bluer than I came." Later she moved to a Mormon colony in Mexico with Frederick and his first wife, Amanda.

Plural marriage had a way of producing strong women. They often had to show great independence in guiding their families without the regular companionship of a husband. Emmeline B. Wells, one of the great women of the era, reared her five daughters in a house apart from her husband, Daniel H. Wells. As her girls approached adulthood, she became editor of the *Woman's Exponent,* a position she held for thirty-seven years. She wrote hundreds of articles, published a book of poetry, represented the Church in national women's conferences, defended the Church before Congress and the President of the United States, and became general president of the Relief Society at age eighty-one. She served until just before her death, more than a decade later.

The children of polygamist families often showed independence and self-will. Susa Young Gates, one of Brigham Young's daughters, took to heart her father's beliefs in equal education for women. She studied at the Brigham Young Academy. She married Jacob Gates and bore eleven children, only four of whom lived to adulthood. She founded and edited the *Young Women's Journal* and served on the general board of the Relief Society. Later she edited the *Relief Society Magazine*. In addition, she wrote poetry, novels, and a biography of her father.

The disruption to the Church, caused by those who opposed plural marriage, was damaging. Many Church leaders, including John Taylor himself, were forced to go into hiding. The women and children kept farms and businesses going as best they could. Programs of expansion, missionary service, immigration—almost all activities of the Church—were crippled.

The day was to come when the very existence of the Church would be threatened. In 1887, President Taylor, who had been in bad health for over a year and was still in hiding, died. Wilford Woodruff, one of the pioneer stalwarts, and certainly one of the greatest missionaries the Church had known, was president of the Quorum of the Twelve. As such, he led the Church until 1889, when he was sustained as President of the Church.

In that same year, the Edmunds-Tucker bill, which was passed in 1887, was taking force. Through this new legislation, the campaign against polygamy now struck at the Church itself. Orders were given that the Church was to be dissolved as a corporation, and all property over $50,000 in value was to be turned over to the government. The Perpetual Emigrating Fund was also dissolved, as was the Mormon militia, still called the Nauvoo Legion. Women were required by law to give evidence against their husbands. The right of women in the territory to vote was taken away; in fact, everyone unwilling to pledge obedience to the anti-polygamy laws was ineligible to vote. Schools were placed under federal control, and the right to perform marriages was limited to probate courts.

Without question, the goal of this legislation was to make continuation of plural marriage impossible. Without financial means, temples could not be completed, and almost all Church programs would be virtually destroyed. By 1890 another law was being proposed in Washington that would take away from every member of the Church the right to vote. All political power in the territory would thus be in the hands of non-Mormons.

President Wilford Woodruff wrestled with the dilemma for many months before he received a revelation from God. He told the Saints: "The Lord showed me by vision and revelation exactly what would take place if we did not stop this practice. . . . He has told me exactly what to do, and what the result would be if we did not do it. . . . I should have let all the temples go out of our hands; I should have gone to prison myself, and let every other man go there, had not the God of Heaven commanded me to do what I did do; and when the hour came that I was commanded to do that, it was all clear to me."

In September 1890, President Woodruff issued a statement, known as the Manifesto. This proclamation stated that the practice of plural marriage was officially ended, and no Latter-day Saints would be allowed to enter it. This was not an admission that the practice was wrong, but merely a statement that the Church would adhere to the laws of the land. On October 6, 1890, the Manifesto was approved by the membership of the Church.

While some people across the nation mistrusted the sincerity of the Saints' action, most accepted the Manifesto as the hoped-for victory. Legally, husbands who continued to support plural wives and their families could still be prosecuted, but judges did not apply that part of the law.

In 1896, Utah was finally admitted to the Union as a state.

The Manifesto opened the way for the Church to resume its programs, but the legislation of the past few years had

Wilford Woodruff

hurt the Church financially, and the 1890s were not easy years. Nonetheless, missionary work went forward, and several new missions were opened.

The great achievement of the era, however, was the completion of the Salt Lake Temple in 1893. Brigham Young had chosen the spot for the temple almost half a decade before, and work on the great granite building had continued for forty years. To the Saints, the temple was a symbol of their perseverance and commitment to the gospel.

CHAPTER 22

The Twentieth Century

In September 1898, President Wilford Woodruff died. Lorenzo Snow, next in line of authority, was eighty-four years old and felt unable to lead the Church. When he received news of President Woodruff's death, he went to the Salt Lake Temple to pray for some manifestation, some instruction as to what he should do. Nothing came. As he walked from his room in the temple, he was deeply disappointed and concerned. Then, in the hallway, a magnificent vision opened before him. Jesus Christ appeared and told him that he should reorganize the First Presidency immediately, not wait as previous presidents had done. Lorenzo Snow had his reassurance.

Despite his doubts about himself, President Snow had been well prepared for this new calling. He had been a member of the Church almost from the beginning, joining at age twenty-two in the year 1836. Through the years, he had served in many ways. He was one of the early missionaries to England and an important leader during the migration to Utah. He became an apostle in 1849 and shortly afterward opened the first mission in Italy. He served other missions throughout the world and was sent to bless Palestine so that

Lorenzo Snow

the way might be opened for the return of the Jews to that land. In Brigham City, Utah, he had organized a successful cooperative that became a model of the cooperative system.

But he was old, and it was not easy for him to understand why the Lord would preserve him to lead the Church. With the end of plural marriage, the Church had been able to get back to its basic purposes, but effects of the financial damage lingered. The Edmunds-Tucker Act had taken from the Church many of its holdings, and legal fees to defend the Church had been expensive. The Saints had seen little reason to pay tithing when the money would end up in the government's hands, so tithing receipts had dwindled.

By 1898, the Church owed well over a million dollars. President Snow decided to issue bonds, which he sold primarily to Latter-day Saints. This bought time by paying off creditors, and it reduced interest rates, but it did not provide a long-term solution. That solution came through inspiration from God.

In the spring of 1899, President Snow felt inspired to go to St. George, Utah. And yet, he was not sure why. As he preached at a special conference in the St. George Tabernacle, suddenly he paused. People saw a strange look come over him and then heard the change in his voice when he began to speak again. What he preached about was tithing—hardly a new idea. But he made a promise to the Saints of southern Utah that if they would pay their tithes—a full ten percent of their income—the disastrous drought in that area would end, and they would prosper.

President Snow and his travel companions stopped at every settlement along the way back to Salt Lake City, and everywhere he preached the same message. And the Saints began to respond. Over the next few weeks tithing began to pour in. But the drought had not ended. President Snow pleaded with the Lord to keep the promise. Then word came: the rains had finally come, and the crops had been saved.

The reversal of the Church's financial position happened quickly. By the time President Snow died in 1901, much of the debt had been paid off, and by 1906 the Church was able to announce complete freedom from debt.

Though Lorenzo Snow's term as President was short, his accomplishments were great. In addition to the reversal in financial matters, various reforms were made in the operation of the programs of the auxiliaries, the educational system, missionary work, and the priesthood quorums. These continued to be the major concerns of Joseph F. Smith, who became President in 1901.

Joseph F. Smith was the nephew of the Prophet, Joseph Smith. He was the baby born to Hyrum and Mary Fielding Smith during those last, terrible days in Far West, when

Joseph F. Smith

Hyrum had been taken off to the Liberty Jail. Young Joseph's father had been martyred when the boy was five.

At nine he had helped his mother drive an ox cart across the plains. During that trek, he learned a great lesson about prayer and faith. One morning he awoke to find a team of oxen gone. He and his uncle Joseph Fielding searched for them for hours and finally gave up. But as the young boy returned to his wagon, he saw his mother on her knees, pleading with the Lord for help in locating the lost animals. When his Uncle Joseph told Mary that all hope was gone, she replied that she would go search for the animals, even though her son and her brother had looked everywhere. As she started off, a man rode up and told her that he had seen the oxen earlier, but in the opposite direction from the one she was walking in. But Mary kept on her original path; she knew where she was going. She walked straight to the oxen.

When Joseph F. was thirteen, his mother died, leaving him orphaned. At fifteen, in 1854, he was called on a mission to Hawaii, then known as the Sandwich Islands, where he learned the language rapidly and served as effectively as grown men. He served for three years and even presided over branches of the Church as a teenager.

By age twenty-seven he had served three missions, and then he was called to be an apostle. In that position he continued his missionary work, serving twice as president of the European Mission. He returned to Hawaii in 1864 to aid the Saints there in a time of crisis, and in the 1880s, during the difficult days when great pressure was on those who practiced plural marriage, he went to Hawaii once again, to escape harassment. He was a tremendous help to the Saints in Hawaii, especially in leadership training and the missionary effort.

In 1886, when the Saints were struggling to keep a Church-sponsored plantation functioning in Laie on the island of Oahu, he prophesied that the day would come when the barren land would be made lush and beautiful. His prophecy came to pass, and the members never forgot it.

As an apostle, Joseph F. Smith toured Church historical sites in the eastern states. Later, during his presidency, he purchased important early properties, such as the Liberty Jail in Missouri and the Joseph Smith home in Sharon, Vermont, beginning the process of preserving the Mormon heritage for future generations.

As Joseph F. Smith took office, he was hopeful of a period of international acceptance of the Church. But the times were difficult. In 1898, Elder B. H. Roberts of the First Council of the Seventy was elected to Congress but was not seated. While an unwritten agreement allowed Mormons to continue to live in plural marriage so long as new marriages were not performed, Congress was not so lenient. Many believed that the Mormons had not really given up the principle.

Four years later Elder Reed Smoot, an apostle, was elected to the United States Senate. The Senate voted to seat him, but for almost five years an investigation continued. He was not a polygamist, but he was accused of being a member of a church that still taught polygamy, and of being part of a religious kingdom that gave ultimate loyalty to church and not to country.

President Smith, partly in response to the investigation, issued a "second manifesto" in 1904, reassuring the nation that the Church no longer taught plural marriage and would excommunicate members who continued the practice. President Smith himself testified before the Senate, promising its members that Senator Smoot was free to vote his own conscience and would not be directed by the Church.

Eventually the Senate seated Senator Smoot, but negative news reports of the hearings had spread throughout the world. Mormon missionaries were often run out of towns, some even beaten or murdered. In England, sensational stories about Mormon missionaries became the basis for a series of cheap novels. Missionaries were portrayed as evil persons who hypnotized young women and dragged them off to Salt Lake City, where they were forced into secret polygamist marriages.

For two decades after the Manifesto, the negative publicity continued. However, toward the end of Joseph F. Smith's presidency, certain events began to turn the tide. Theodore Roosevelt, former President of the United States, and Winston Churchill, Home Secretary in England, both spoke out on behalf of the Church.

About the same time, a visitors' center was established on Temple Square in Salt Lake City. Thousands of tourists began to hear the Church's point of view concerning its history and doctrine. The Tabernacle Choir was becoming famous and was invited to sing in the East. Reed Smoot became a respected member of Congress, noted for his hard work. And between 1909 and 1915, *Americana Magazine* published the detailed account of Mormon history written by B. H. Roberts.

President Smith taught the Mormons throughout the world to build up the Church in their own areas and not to think about gathering to Utah. This was a major change in thinking for the Saints. For three-quarters of a century, the great stress had been on gathering. But Joseph Smith had always taught that Zion would be a central place from which the gospel would go to all the world. And now the time had come to extend Zion, to strengthen the Church in all the lands of the earth.

President Smith traveled to Europe in 1906 and again in 1910. He was the first President to visit there while in office. The Saints in the areas he visited were greatly moved by the personal attention of their prophet. In Rotterdam, Holland, a blind eleven-year-old boy expressed his faith that President Smith "had the most power of any missionary on earth. If he will look into my eyes," the boy said, "I believe they will be healed." And indeed, the boy's eyes were healed, through the faith of the prophet and the faith of the boy.

While attending a conference in Bern, Switzerland, President Smith told the Saints that the day would come when many temples would be built in Europe and in "diverse countries." It would be many years before this prophecy would begin to take place, but when it did, the first European temple was built near Bern.

President Smith visited his beloved Hawaii four times while in office. Missionary work had continued over the years not only in the Hawaiian islands, but also in islands throughout the Pacific—New Zealand, Tahiti, Samoa, Tonga, Fiji, and other areas.

In 1915, President Smith could see the great need for a temple for the peoples of these islands. While visiting Laie, on the island of Oahu, he went for a stroll one evening. He told Elder Reed Smoot, who had accompanied him to the islands, "I feel impressed to dedicate this ground for the erection of a Temple of God, for a place where the peoples of the Pacific Isles can come and do their temple work. I have not presented this to the Council of the Twelve or to my counselors; but if you think there would be no objection to it, I think now is the time to dedicate the ground."

Elder Smoot later said, "Never in all my life did I hear such a prayer. The very ground seemed to be sacred, and he seemed as if he were talking face to face with the Father. I cannot and never will forget it if I live a thousand years." The temple was begun in 1916 and dedicated in 1919. President Smith would not live to see it completed for he died in 1918.

President Smith also took an interest in Canada and Mexico, places where the Church was most prominent outside the United States. He told the Canadian Saints in Alberta Province that it was time that they had access to a temple. In 1913 he dedicated land for a temple in Cardston, and the construction began soon after. The building was dedicated in 1923.

Another important event of President Smith's administration was the first World War. For the first time Latter-day Saints were fighting against each other, on both sides of the war. The Church wrestled with the difficult problem and took the position that would again be taken in World War II. Members should honor the governments of their own countries and not resist, but they should also do everything within their power to turn their service into an opportunity to preach the gospel.

As it turned out, the war did give the Saints a chance to make positive contributions. In the United States and En-

gland, the response of Mormon volunteers proved their loyalty to country, a loyalty that had previously been doubted.
Also, the work of the Relief Society in getting food and
clothing to the afflicted people of Europe was widely pub-
licized and praised. Both helped improve the Church's
image. In President Smith's last years, he took strong stands
on moral issues, preaching such basic principles as adher-
ence to the Word of Wisdom, chastity, diligence, and industry. He also solidified the Church's financial position by
making investments in such industries as sugar, banking, in-
surance, publications, and retailing. He built the beautiful
Hotel Utah for investment purposes, and also approved construction of other important Church buildings, including
the Church Administration Building.

Just a few days after the end of World War I, Joseph F.
Smith died. In his time, the Church had shaken off many of
the negative images of the past, taken the first steps toward
becoming a worldwide church, and made a great leap into
the modern world.

CHAPTER 23

The Depression and World War II

Heber J. Grant became President of the Church in 1918. He was the first President who had not lived through the Missouri and Illinois trials of the Church. He was born in Utah in 1856.

Heber's father, Jedediah M. Grant, was the first mayor of Salt Lake City and died just nine days after Heber's birth. His mother, Rachel, worked hard to support herself and her son by sewing and taking in boarders. Heber also helped. He was devoted to accomplishing the things he set out to do. He made up his mind to improve his penmanship and developed beautiful handwriting, through much practice. He practiced throwing a baseball against his Bishop's barn until his arm would ache so badly he "scarcely could go to sleep at night." But he reached his goal: he played for the territorial champion baseball team.

At age twenty-three he was called by the First Presidency to move to Tooele, Utah, to serve as stake president. Two years later, in 1882, he was almost overwhelmed when he was called to serve in the Quorum of the Twelve Apostles.

Heber J. Grant

He was a member of the Twelve for thirty-six years, until President Joseph F. Smith's death in 1918. President Grant was the last President of the Church to practice plural marriage; his three wives bore him ten daughters to whom he was greatly devoted.

An outgoing, friendly man, Heber J. Grant had a wide circle of friends both in and out of the Church. He liked to talk over business matters pertaining to the Church during a game of golf, and he tried to get some physical exercise every day. He was to preside over the Church for twenty-seven years, longer than any other President but Brigham Young.

Shortly after President Grant took office, Church membership passed the half million mark. Most of these members still lived in the Intermountain West. During his administration, the population of the Church began to move outward. During the financially difficult times of the Great Depression, many Latter-day Saints in the Great Basin, especially young people, moved to other regions to find work. Missionary work also continued to build the strength of the Church throughout the world. The first stake organized outside the Great Basin was established in Los Angeles in 1923, and over the next few years many others were created. From 1920 to 1940, membership in California grew from 2.8 to 10.9 percent of the total Church membership.

President Grant was committed to establishing and building in all parts of the world. In 1920, he sent Elder David O. McKay of the Quorum of the Twelve on a 56,000-mile tour of missions, seeking a clearer knowledge of how missionary work could be moved forward. The tour lasted thirteen months and took Elder McKay to the many Pacific Islands, to China (where he dedicated that land for eventual missionary work), to Southeast Asia, to the Holy Land, and to the missions in Europe.

Elder McKay was especially moved by his experiences in the islands. He had never met such loving or faithful people. In New Zealand he spoke at a special conference, where most of the audience was Maori. He told them, "Oh, how I wish I could speak to you in your own language to tell you what is in my heart, but since I cannot, I am going to pray that while I speak in my own tongue you may have the gift of interpretation and discernment." And then a miracle occurred. A missionary who was there told the story:

"He spoke several sentences and then Stuart [Meha] would interpret into Maori. Then he'd make another statement in English and Stuart would interpret. All at once everything was quiet, and all over the congregation the Maoris—not the Europeans but the Maoris—called out, 'Stuart, sit down, don't interpret; we can understand what the Apostle is saying.'"

When Elder McKay returned to Salt Lake City, he was able to give President Grant and other leaders a clearer picture of the state of the Church throughout the world. In Europe and in the Pacific islands, there was reason for great hope. But the Orient, as of yet, showed little progress. In other parts of the world, such as eastern Europe, South America, and Africa, missionary work was still slow or not yet established.

The Church was expanding, but the work of taking the gospel to all the world was only just beginning. Commitment to that purpose was a high priority to President Grant. In a conference address, he told the Saints, "It is our duty above all others to go forth and proclaim the gospel of the Lord Jesus Christ." He followed up on this commitment by increasing the number of missions and missionaries.

In the early years of the twentieth century, the Church closed most of its elementary schools and academies, or high schools. To provide religious instruction for the youth, seminaries were established to teach religion courses to high-school students during released time from school or in the early morning hours before school. President Grant also committed the Church to developing Brigham Young University as a major institution of higher learning. By the 1930s, the only other colleges operated by the Church were Ricks College in Rexburg, Idaho, and the LDS Business College and the McCune School of Music in Salt Lake City. To provide religious instruction for college students, institutes of religion were opened at major colleges in the western states where large numbers of LDS students were enrolled.

The Great Depression, which began in 1929 and continued through the 1930s, was devastating to Latter-day Saints as well as other Americans. But out of it came the development of a unique program that would provide work, food, and clothing for the needy and would bring widespread recognition to the Church.

In a stake in one of the poorer sections of Salt Lake City, Harold B. Lee, the stake president, developed a welfare program for his stake that would become the basis for a Churchwide welfare plan. Under this program, cooperative farms, canneries, and small factories were established to produce food and other items needed by the Saints. These were taken to central distribution centers, where they were given to the needy. All members of the Church, rich and poor alike, were encouraged to participate in projects to help care for those in need as well as provide for their own families. The Church encouraged the Saints to store food and other staple products for use in times of crisis; to plant vegetable gardens; to avoid debt; and to get vocational training and education.

President Lee was called in 1936 to oversee the welfare program for the Church, and in 1941, he became a member of the Quorum of the Twelve Apostles. Through the welfare efforts of the Saints, thousands of Latter-day Saints were able to go off government relief programs, and many thousands more were assisted.

World War II broke out in Europe in 1939, and in 1941 the United States was drawn in, with fighting in Europe and the South Pacific and Asia. The war brought an end to the depression, but it required new kinds of commitment. Once again the Church was caught in the dilemma of member fighting member in a worldwide conflict. But the message of the gospel was spread in ways that it otherwise might not have been. Mormon servicemen introduced the gospel in new lands, and many new converts were made. By the time the war ended, The Church of Jesus Christ of Latter-day Saints had entered into a very different era, one that would see doors opening up for great worldwide expansion.

Heber J. Grant had become President of the Church in November 1918, at the end of World War I. As World War

II was coming to a close in May of 1945, he died. He was succeeded by George Albert Smith, a grandson of George A. Smith, the boy who had marched with the Prophet Joseph Smith in Zion's Camp. His father was John Henry Smith, who had served as an apostle and member of the First Presidency.

At age twenty-two, George Albert Smith married Emily Woodruff, granddaughter of President Wilford Woodruff. A month later he left to serve a mission to the southern states. At thirty-three he was called as an apostle. He served as president of the European Mission immediately after World War I, which prepared him for the special challenges as leader of the Church in another post-war period.

President Smith was active in Boy Scouts and a great supporter of youth programs. During his apostleship he presided over the Young Men's Mutual Improvement Associa-

George Albert Smith

tion, and in 1932 he was elected to the national executive committee of Boy Scouts of America. He was also active in locating and preserving Mormon historic sites.

President Smith's most notable quality, according to those who knew him, was his gentle manner and Christlike love. He carried that spirit into the First Presidency, along with great energy to get many programs of the Church, slowed by the war, back into full activity.

Shortly after the end of the fighting, President Smith paid a visit to U.S. President Harry S Truman. The Church wanted to ship food, clothing, blankets, and other items to Mormons in Europe. President Truman was impressed by the sentiment but wondered how long it would take. "It is all ready," was the response. President Truman was astounded. In a time when most Americans were concentrating on their own recovery from the strains of war, the Mormons had begun to think of their brothers and sisters who were worse off in Europe.

In January 1946 Elder Ezra Taft Benson of the Council of the Twelve traveled to Europe to supervise the distribution of the supplies. He was the first American civilian authorized to travel through all four occupied zones of Germany. He also traveled throughout the other devastated countries across the continent. Transportation and communication had been cut off in many places, and the large cities had been extensively bombed. Latter-day Saints, however, had stayed in contact with one another and had held meetings during the war when they could. When Elder Benson arrived, the Saints were very thankful for the clothing and food, but they were just as thrilled to have renewed contact with the Church leaders.

Typical of Elder Benson's experience in Europe was a meeting in Karlsruhe, Germany. He had been delayed in arriving there and was not certain where the meeting was to be held. He walked through the streets and climbed over rubble, looking for the meeting place. Then he heard a congregation singing in the distance: the hymn was "Come, Come Ye Saints." In a bombed-out building, 260 Saints had waited for Elder Benson to arrive. He reported:

"For the first time in my life, I saw almost an entire audience in tears as we walked up onto the platform, and they realized that at last, after six or seven long years, representatives from Zion, as they put it, had finally come back among them. Then as the meeting closed, . . . they insisted that we go to the door and shake hands with each of them as we left the bombed-out building. And we noted that many of them, after they had passed through the line, went back and came through a second and third time, so happy were they to grasp our hands. As I looked into their upturned faces, pale, thin, many of these Saints dressed in rags, some of them barefooted, I could see the light of faith in their eyes as they bore testimony of the divinity of this great latter-day work, and expressed their gratitude for the blessings of the Lord."

The war had slowed missionary work drastically, with so many young men serving in the armed forces rather than on missions, preaching, but many Mormon soldiers took the spirit of missionary work with them. They converted military friends, and they taught the natives in such places as the Philippines and other islands of the Pacific.

The war had shut down many activities in the United States as well. To conserve energy, meetings and social events were curtailed. Almost all building was halted, including the construction of a temple in Idaho Falls, Idaho. President Smith now pushed to see the work of the Church return to full speed.

Missionary work increased, with new missions opening. Many soldiers returned home, exchanged uniforms for suits, and left home again to serve the Lord.

CHAPTER 24

The Worldwide Church

In 1947, the Church celebrated the centennial of the pioneers' arrival in the Salt Lake Valley. The "This Is the Place" monument was dedicated near the site where Brigham Young had first entered the valley. Cars fitted out to look like covered wagons retraced the trek of the pioneers to Utah, and President George Albert Smith joined them for the last few miles.

In one hundred years, the Saints had put down powerful roots, and now the branches of the tree could spread. With the war over, new opportunities for missionary work were open. At last the Saints were receiving favorable publicity throughout most of the world. This had begun with the Church's welfare accomplishments in the depression and now continued with the aid to Europe at war's end. Broadcasts of the Tabernacle Choir had continued during the war, and the choir was now making recordings that actually placed high on hit charts. The Mormons were being accepted as part of American culture in ways they had never before imagined.

George Albert Smith died on his eighty-first birthday, in April 1951. He had seen great strides in the six years he led the Church. But even he could probably not have predicted

David O. McKay

the incredible growth of the Church that was about to begin.

David O. McKay, who became the ninth President of the Church, was an educator and the first college graduate to serve as prophet, seer, and revelator. He was raised in the small town of Huntsville, Utah. He had learned to take responsibility at an early age. When he was seven, his father was called on a mission. His two older sisters had recently died, and David's mother was expecting another baby. David, the oldest son, took on many of the household chores and responsibilities.

As he grew up, he strove to acquire a testimony of the gospel and to prepare himself for a productive career in teaching. He attended the University of Utah and was president and valedictorian of his class. After graduation, he served a mission to Great Britain. Following his mission, David taught at the Weber Stake Academy in Ogden, Utah, and soon became principal of the school. At the same time, he was called by Weber Stake to prepare a program of instruction for Sunday School. Eventually his techniques for teaching the gospel were used throughout the Church.

In 1906, at age thirty-two, David O. McKay was called to serve as an apostle. The Church continued to use his educational skills, appointing him general superintendent of the Sunday School and Church Commissioner of Education. In December 1920 he left for a one-year worldwide tour of missions, and soon after his return, he became president of the European Mission. From 1934 to 1951, he was a member of the First Presidency.

On April 9, 1951, at age seventy-seven, he became President of the Church. During the next two decades the membership grew so rapidly that the majority of the Saints had never known another president. In 1947 the Church had passed the one-million-member mark; by 1970, the year of President McKay's death, the membership was almost three million. When he became president, 184 stakes existed; on the day he died, the five hundredth stake was organized.

Perhaps most telling of all, the Church's membership was no longer primarily in the western part of the United States. Great growth was seen in the rest of the nation. And while Europe had been a fruitful field for missionary labors in earlier years, the conversion rate increased at a very rapid pace in Latin America and the Far East. What made all this progress especially surprising was that missionary efforts were temporarily slowed by war in Korea in the early 1950s.

The growth in membership created tremendous needs for new chapels and temples throughout the world. From 1946 to 1955, 1,350 Church buildings were constructed, and the numbers continued to grow from that point. In

1965, 556 chapels were under construction at the same time.

During the 1950s, temples were completed and dedicated in Switzerland, Los Angeles, England, and New Zealand, and in 1964 the Oakland Temple, overlooking San Francisco Bay, was dedicated.

The Latter-day Saint commitment to education was also evident. Brigham Young University grew from fewer than 6,000 students to almost 26,000. Seminary and institute programs expanded to many new areas, with early-morning seminary introduced in places where release-time programs were not possible. In 1958 a college was opened in Laie, Hawaii. Now known as Brigham Young University–Hawaii Campus, it was established to give Latter-day Saints throughout the Pacific an opportunity to receive college training. This was the fulfillment of the vision President McKay had had many years before during his first tour of the islands.

In Mexico and some South American nations, where young members were receiving little or no opportunity for schooling, the Church established several elementary and high schools.

More than ever before, Mormons became prominent in virtually every field of endeavor: in science, entertainment, medicine, sports, politics, and many other areas. Ezra Taft Benson, a member of the Council of the Twelve Apostles, became Secretary of Agriculture under President Dwight D. Eisenhower. J. Reuben Clark, a member of the First Presidency, had served as American ambassador to Mexico.

With the Church growing so rapidly, and with such diversity of cultures, languages, and national heritages now represented in the membership, certain adjustments were becoming necessary to maintain order and consistency. Modern technology in communication, travel, and record storage helped to deal with some of the challenges. It became clear, however, that additional efforts were needed to coordinate Church programs.

Harold B. Lee, the apostle who had directed the welfare program during the Great Depression, became chairman of a new correlation committee to coordinate all of the priesthood, auxiliary, and nonreligious programs. The family was placed at the center of all gospel instruction, with the priesthood given added responsibility in directing affairs of the Church.

The many changes introduced in the 1970s could have placed the Church in danger of becoming a great bureaucracy, distant from the early spiritual community associated with Mormonism. But, in fact, membership involvement continued to increase and commitment was at a high level. Church attendance, missionary work, temple work, youth involvement, and paying of tithes all increased during this period of rapid expansion.

David O. McKay died in 1970, and Joseph Fielding Smith, a son of President Joseph F. Smith and a grandson of

Joseph Fielding Smith

Hyrum Smith, the Prophet's brother, became the President. He was ninety-three years old. He was perhaps best known for his gospel scholarship, but he also had a great spirit of love and kindness. He served as President for only thirty months, but during that time he won the hearts of the Saints.

Joseph Fielding had devoted much of his life to research and writing. All of his adult life was given to Church work of one kind or another. He was a member of the Council of the Twelve Apostles for nearly sixty years, and served as Church Historian for forty-nine of those years. While he worked with genealogical and historical assignments, he published many books on Church history and doctrine.

When Joseph Fielding Smith died in 1972, the much younger Harold B. Lee became President. His success in de-

Harold B. Lee

veloping the welfare system of the Church and in correlating Church programs had prepared him well. But to the surprise and sadness of Church members, he died after only a year and a half in office, in December 1973.

Though their terms of office were short, both Joseph Fielding Smith and Harold B. Lee continued to direct the correlation and consolidation programs begun under President McKay's direction. The Church grew at the same rapid pace, and the challenge of reaching all members in such diversified areas meant almost constant review and updating of Church activities.

Perhaps the greatest symbol of the time was that Latter-day Saints in many parts of the world could now watch or at least listen to general conferences—still held in the beautiful old pioneer tabernacle on Temple Square. Television networks took the broadcasts across the continent, and radio extended the audience to other continents as well. Eventually satellite systems would make the conference sessions more readily available.

But it was one thing for the message of the gospel to reach around the world; it was another for all members to feel a spirit of love for each other. That challenge grew as the Church increased in size and diversity. Time and again, however, the Saints found that the power of the Spirit could transcend cultural, racial, and national differences.

The story of Frank Day typified the experience of many Mormons. He had been an American soldier, a Marine, in World War II and had come to hate the Japanese, America's enemies in that war. He had harbored these feelings—not just for the Japanese but for all Orientals—for more than two decades after the war. Then, as an administrator of the Church Educational System, he was assigned to supervise programs in the Orient and Pacific islands.

Brother Day was frustrated and upset. "I seriously won-

dered how I could sit with the Orientals," he said. He flew to
Okinawa, the very city where he had been stationed immediately after the war.

At the airport, he was met by the mission president. He
later reported: "As I took two or three steps toward the mission president, the Japanese brother, it was one of the
most unusual experiences I think I'll ever have, because in a
matter of seconds, the bitterness and the hatred, the training and fear of years, was suddenly eliminated. I stepped up
and it was the most natural thing in the world to put my arms
around Brother Kan Watanabe, the mission president. He
put his arms around me and all of the hatred was gone and a
love of the Oriental was instilled in me at that time as he
said, 'Welcome to Okinawa.' Since that day, the only answer that I can give is that the Lord stepped in to assist and
the enmity was taken away, completely wiped out."

During that visit, Brother Day presided over a meeting
that brought together Church members from Japan, Korea,
Taiwan, Hong Kong, and the Philippines. Some of the
nations these men represented had been enemies not only in
World War II, but for centuries. Brother Day said: "At the
conclusion of this convention the Japanese coordinator and
the Korean coordinator, who had backgrounds that should
have required in their own feelings that they not even be in
the same room, put their arms around each other and I heard
the Japanese say to the Korean, 'Thank you so much for all
you've done for us in this convention. I want you to know
that I love you with all my heart.'"

Similar experiences were reported in Europe, where
members from many European countries that had been on
opposite sides expressed their love for one another. In the
Pacific, Saints from many islands have gone to Laie, Hawaii,
for education and to work at the Polynesian Cultural Center, where diversity is honored and cultural differences are

enjoyed. In the western United States, old prejudices against Indians have been overcome as families have accepted Indian children into their homes and helped them get an education. Latin, Indian, and European cultures have also come together throughout South America.

Such accomplishments are evidence of what the gospel of Jesus Christ can do to help bridge differences between people and nations.

CHAPTER 25

The Modern Church

When Spencer W. Kimball became President of the Church in late 1973, many members expected another short presidency. Though he was seventy-eight, younger than some of the previous prophets, he had experienced numerous health problems in his life. But Spencer Kimball had been strengthened, not weakened by his many ordeals. And when he called for the Saints to lengthen their stride, they soon learned that he himself could walk very fast indeed.

President Kimball's tests had begun early in life when he was growing up in Arizona. His mother died when he was eleven, and he felt the loss deeply. He could have seen his size (he was not much over five feet tall) as a handicap, but he became a star in what is today a tall person's sport: basketball. After serving a mission in the Central States, he married Camilla Eyring and began a career in banking and real estate. He became a stake clerk at the age of twenty-three and then served in a stake presidency. He was a stake president in Safford, Arizona, when he received a call to serve as an apostle in 1943.

After joining the Quorum of the Twelve, he experienced a series of heart attacks that slowed him temporarily,

Spencer W. Kimball with Chief Dan George

but he always bounced back with an enthusiasm and commitment that few could match. He became the champion of Indians and other minorities, and he was always reaching out to those who suffered. His book *The Miracle of Forgiveness* became one of the most widely read books in the Church.

In 1957 President Kimball underwent surgery for cancer of the throat. Very little was left of his voice. He worked hard, however, to rebuild his ability to speak. Eventually, though his former voice was gone, a soft voice developed in its place. But his trials were not over. In 1972 he underwent open-heart surgery. He was still regaining his strength when President Lee died. He was shocked by the death, frightened that he was not the man to lead in such challenging times. As usual, however, he went at the work with full intensity and was soon moving the Church to unexpected accomplishments.

"We must lengthen our stride" became President Kimball's motto. The Church must be taken to all the earth, and that meant that more missionaries must be called. Temple work must be increased, taking advantage of modern technology. The members must live the gospel as never before, setting an example to all the world.

Within a few years the army of missionaries had grown dramatically, with more young Mormon men and women accepting calls than ever before. Many retired couples also entered the mission field. A large complex of buildings, the Missionary Training Center, was constructed near the Brigham Young University campus so that the missionaries would be well prepared.

The Church grew dramatically as the missionary effort was increased. Between 1830 and 1970, a period of 140 years, 500 stakes had been created. From 1970 to 1979, a period of only nine years, another 500 were added. The one-thousandth stake was established, fittingly, in Nauvoo, Illinois. Since then, the number of new stakes created has continued at a similar pace.

In the 1960s and 1970s, convert baptisms in Mexico, Central America, and South America exploded. By 1977 there were more Church members in Mexico City than in Ogden or Provo, Utah, two of the largest cities close to Church headquarters. On one weekend in November 1977, five stakes in Mexico City were divided into fifteen.

Another symbol of growth in the Church has been the expansion of temple work. When President Kimball became President, there were fifteen temples, with a sixteenth under construction. But President Kimball saw the need for members in many parts of the world to have an opportunity to receive their endowments and perform work for their kindred dead. In 1974 the first temple in the eastern United States was completed in Washington, D.C. In 1975 plans for three new temples were announced: the first ever in

South America, at Sao Paulo, Brazil; the first in Asia, at Tokyo, Japan; and the first in the northwestern United States, near Seattle, Washington.

But this was only the beginning. In the next few years many more plans were announced, bringing temples to many parts of the United States and to such lands as Argentina, Chile, Australia, Tonga, Tahiti, Western Samoa, West Germany, and, most surprisingly, East Germany. By the late 1980s there will be almost fifty temples in operation or being built.

At the same time, a name extraction program, under which genealogical missionaries go throughout the world to microfilm birth, death, marriage, and other records, has expanded the number of names available to keep pace with the increase in temple work.

In 1975 President Kimball reorganized the First Quorum of Seventy, as in the days of Joseph Smith. This body of priesthood leaders has assumed many responsibilities in leading the programs and missionary work of the Church.

One of President Kimball's most important actions came in 1978. For many years the Church had been criticized for withholding priesthood ordination from black members, a policy that had been in effect since the early days of the Church. President Kimball, who had long been a champion of minorities, sought the Lord's will on this matter. In June 1978, he announced that he had received a revelation that the time had come for all worthy male members to receive the blessing of the priesthood.

This change in policy opened up broader missionary possibilities. Black members could now receive the blessings of the temple endowment and assume positions of leadership. Latter-day Saints everywhere were thrilled as the announcement was spread around the world in all the news media. The strength of Mormonism had always been in its belief in continued revelation, and here was evidence of that great blessing.

President Kimball died in November 1985 at age ninety. At the end of that year, the Church membership was 5,920,000. It had more than doubled since the death of President David O. McKay in 1970, just fifteen years earlier. At the end of 1985, there were 1,582 stakes with 12,934 wards. Nearly two hundred thousand convert baptisms were performed in 1985, compared with 79,126 in 1970.

Ezra Taft Benson was ordained as the thirteenth President of the Church in November 1985, at age eighty-six. He had been a member of the Council of the Twelve Apostles since 1943 and had served as president of that quorum since 1973.

President Benson's rich background, from farm boy to U.S. Secretary of Agriculture, from deacon to apostle, had prepared him well. It was he who had gone to Europe after

Ezra Taft Benson

World War II to help reopen the missions and distribute food and clothing to the Saints. He had also served as president of the Quorum of the Twelve under President Kimball, helping to direct the expansion of the Church in the 1970s and early 1980s.

At a press conference following his ordination, President Benson expressed his love to all people of the world, "of every color, creed, or political persuasion."

And so, as the Church passed into the second half of the 1980s, its strength had never been more clear, and the public image had never been better. But challenges remained.

No longer can Church members think of themselves as a single culture. The Church now includes members of many languages, nationalities, political backgrounds, and cultural heritages. Such diversity requires special sensitivity and care. A Christian spirit of acceptance and understanding is needed more than ever before.

Elder Bruce R. McConkie of the Quorum of the Twelve Apostles spoke to a group of returned missionaries at a gathering in Provo, Utah, in the 1970s. He commented on the openness that is necessary in our time: "Our customs are good for us and we have been trained in them. It is no different to have different languages. You speak the language you inherit. And the Lord knows all languages. As far as he is concerned, it is just as good to speak Mandarin as it is to speak English. On this basis, we are only trying to take truth to people in addition to what they have. . . . Whatever is appropriate and good we want to preserve."

What is true for the Church in America is true for the Church throughout the world. Today Mormon missionaries criss-cross the globe. Europeans, Asians, and South Americans are knocking on doors in Utah as well as in their home countries. The Saints are learning to live together and to love each other and each other's backgrounds.

Church Office
Building,
Salt Lake City

A church of six million members is a quite different organization from the six who met to organize The Church of
Jesus Christ of Latter-day Saints in 1830. Early Latter-day
Saints were close to the Prophet Joseph Smith and were
moved by his charismatic personality. Today most members
never come close enough to see the prophet in person, never
shake his hand. But the Church has not lost the personal
touch, the attention to individual needs.

Mormons are no longer being driven from their homes or
forced to flee for safety, nor are they called to cross the plains
to gather to Zion. Times have changed, and the Church's
programs have changed with them, using new technologies
and ways to accomplish the work of the Lord. The modern
era demands of all a lengthened stride, increased commitment, and the same faith that brought pioneer Mormons
through all their ordeals.

But the basic truths, the truths for which the Saints have sacrificed for more than a century and a half, remain: Jesus Christ himself directed and authorized the organization of his church on earth in these latter days. He continues to guide his church through living prophets. And the Saints will continue to take this message, a message of great joy, to the ends of the earth.

Books for Further Study
in Mormon History

Alexander, Thomas G. *Mormonism in Transition: A History of the Latter-day Saints, 1890-1930.* Urbana, Illinois: University of Illinois Press, 1986.

Alexander, Thomas G., and James B. Allen. *Mormons and Gentiles: A History of Salt Lake City.* Boulder, Colorado: Pruett, 1984.

Allen, James B., and Glen M. Leonard. *The Story of the Latter-day Saints.* Salt Lake City: Deseret Book, 1976.

Arrington, Leonard J. *Brigham Young: American Moses.* New York: Alfred A. Knopf, 1985.

Arrington, Leonard J. *Great Basin Kingdom: An Economic History of the Latter-day Saints, 1830-1900.* Cambridge, Massachusetts: Harvard University Press, 1985.

Arrington, Leonard J., and Davis Bitton. *Saints without Halos: The Human Side of Mormon History.* Salt Lake City: Signature Books, 1981.

Arrington, Leonard J., Feramorz Y. Fox, and Dean L. May. *Building the City of God: Community and Cooperation among the Mormons.* Salt Lake City: Deseret Book, 1976.

Arrington, Leonard J., and Susan Arrington Madsen. *Sunbonnet Sisters: True Stories of Women and Frontier Life.* Salt Lake City: Bookcraft, 1984.

Backman, Milton V. *The Heavens Resound: A History of the Latterday Saints in Ohio, 1830-1838.* Salt Lake City: Deseret Book, 1983.

Barrett, Ivan J. *Joseph Smith and the Restoration*. Provo, Utah: Brigham Young University Press, 1973.

Berrett, William E. *The Latter-day Saints: A Contemporary History*. Salt Lake City: Deseret Book, 1985.

Britsch, R. Lanier. *Unto the Islands of the Sea: A History of the Latter-day Saints in the Pacific*. Salt Lake City: Deseret Book, 1986.

Bushman, Richard L. *Joseph Smith and the Beginnings of Mormonism*. Urbana, Illinois: University of Illinois Press, 1984.

Cowan, Richard O. *The Church in the Twentieth Century*. Salt Lake City: Bookcraft, 1985.

England, Eugene. *Brother Brigham*. Salt Lake City: Publishers Press, 1980.

Flanders, Robert Bruce. *Nauvoo: Kingdom on the Mississippi*. Urbana, Illinois: University of Illinois Press, 1965.

Godfrey, Audrey M., Kenneth M. Godfrey, and Jill Mulvay Derr. *Women's Voices: An Untold History of the Latter-day Saints*. Salt Lake City: Deseret Book, 1982.

Hill, Donna. *Joseph Smith, the First Mormon*. Garden City, New York: Doubleday, 1977.

Newell, Linda King, and Valeen Tippets Avery. *Mormon Enigma: Emma Hale Smith*. Garden City, New York: Doubleday, 1984.

Palmer, Spencer J. *The Expanding Church*. Salt Lake City: Deseret Book, 1978.

Pratt, Parley P. *The Autobiography of Parley P. Pratt*. Salt Lake City: Deseret Book, 1938, 1985.

Roberts, B. H. *A Comprehensive History of The Church of Jesus Christ of Latter-day Saints*. 6 vols. Provo, Utah: Brigham Young University Press, 1965.

Shipp, Ellis Reynolds. *While Others Slept: Autobiography and Journal of Ellis Reynolds Shipp, M.D.* Salt Lake City: Bookcraft, 1985.

Smith, Joseph, Jr. *History of The Church of Jesus Christ of Latter-day Saints*. Salt Lake City: Deseret Book, 1971.

Smith, Joseph Fielding. *Essentials in Church History*. Salt Lake City: Deseret Book, 1973.

Smith, Lucy Mack, with notes and comments by Preston Nibley. *History of Joseph Smith by His Mother*. Salt Lake City: Bookcraft, 1958.

Stout, Hosea, ed. Juanita Brooks. *On the Mormon Frontier: The Diary of Hosea Stout*. Salt Lake City: University of Utah Press, 1964.

Index